ONE MIGHTY TALE

A shooting and fishing life,
through the eyes of a reformed poacher.

by
Martin Grennan

Acknowledgement

Marian,
Your proof reading was great,
your encouragement invaluable.
Thank you.

Published by:
Brook Field Press
E-mail: grennan@eircom.net
Tel: 086-4046326

ISBN 0-9547389-0-X

Designed and Printed by:
Modern Printers, Kilkenny
Tel: 056-7721739

Martin Grennan grew up on a small farm near the village of Rhode in Co. Offaly. In this idyllic, rural setting his boyhood was divided between playing Gaelic football, with some success, for that famous parish and roaming the countryside in search of birds' nests.

Shooting and fishing became the two great sporting loves of his life. Having finished school, he lived for nine years in the bright lights of London before returning to his now adopted county of Kilkenny. Here, as a member of the Callan and District Gun Club, he enjoyed superb shooting, mainly pheasant with some duck, and regular trips to the mountains in search of the elusive grouse. He also travels regularly to Glin on the Shannon estuary, for wild-fowling in the adopted home of his brother Catch.

A member of Kilkenny Anglers' Association, he regularly fishes the beautiful river Nore and its tributaries for both salmon and trout. Dapping the Mayfly takes him on regular jaunts to Oughterard on the shores of Lough Corrib.

Writing, as a hobby, began when his penchant for storytelling became evident. For three years he wrote regular columns for the Irish Shooters Digest and Irish Anglers Digest. Those articles, sometimes nostalgic, sometimes pertinent to the current climate, were invariably humorous.

"One Mighty Tale" is a pleasant mixture of happy, sad and funny memories of his lifelong association with hunting in all its many forms.

Dedication

To my late father, Johnny.

While pheasants fly and trout swim,
your spirit will live on.

CHAPTER ONE

One of my earliest childhood memories is of my father eating breakfast before daylight on a winter's morning. His gun and fowling bag standing ready by the door, gave clear testimony to his intentions. My two older brothers, Kevin and Catch, were already outside putting Grouse, our black and white setter, in the car. Nuala, my older sister, and I were clambering on Daddy's knees to steal a kiss and, hopefully, the top of his egg. Moments later, while Nuala gabbled excitedly about what game we would play for the day, I watched longingly as Daddy picked up his gun and bag and left to go fowling. From that moment, I'd say it was inevitable that I would follow in his footsteps.

It was probably about two years later that I had my first attempt at hunting. This time it was a pleasant early summer day and I idly strolled through the meadow of the brook field intending simply to amuse myself by jumping the drain from which the field took it's name. This was the early days of television and that little brook held for me all the wonders of "The Everglades" and "Voyage To The Bottom Of The Sea" rolled into one. As I reached the bank of the stream, I startled and was startled by the sudden flutter of a cock pheasant, which had been lying contentedly under a whin bush. I saw immediately the indentation in the grass and decided this was what the stupid bird called home. A great plan formed in my childish mind, and as I raced back to the farmyard, in my mind's eye I could already see the weapon I would use, standing as always in the cowshed - a simple ash plant. Standard equipment of Midland farmers for herding cattle,

5

though I've not seen them in my adopted County. Down here, they allow them grow up to be hurleys. I knew it would be only a matter of time before that silly bird got over it's fright and returned to it's 'nest'. I waited for what seemed like ages but was probably about five minutes and crawled back through the meadow, not even daring to talk to myself. A habit I've never quite gotten rid of and see no real need to. When I reached that little whin bush I pounced suddenly, flailing the ash plant for all I was worth, only to find the bird was not quite as stupid as I'd hoped.

Undaunted, I returned to the farm, believing that more time was all that was needed. Twice more that day I returned, each time with the same caution, each time with the same result. I resolved to try again on the morrow and waited for my two brothers to return from whatever jaunt they were on, to tell them of my near miss. When finally they did return and hear the story, their mirthful laughter became for me the first indication that perhaps there was more to capturing game than I had yet imagined.

When Kevin, my eldest brother, attained the great status of manhood – 'leaving school' – and taking up a job, Catch and I became somewhat unlikely partners. There was a five year age gap, which over the years proved to be probably more of a help than a hindrance; my perspective only. His knowledge and experience, to me, were vast and invaluable and his patience, if sometimes suspect, did bring rewards. In those distant days one of my most valuable possessions, in common with most small boys, was a penknife. This could be used for all sorts; paring sticks to make bows and arrows, forkie sticks for catapults, cribs and, in an emergency, it would even kill an Indian. How well I remember the hours spent searching the hedges looking for suitably forked branches to be cut down for the great weapon of the time - a catapult. I still vividly remember our disappointment when red rubber car tubes were replaced with the black ones. We still made catapults, but never again as good.

Often in latter years while shooting, we would find ourselves on either side of a ditch waiting for a pheasant to flush and would be instantly transported back in time to those early days when we stalked small game. In the early days my idea of success was to see a stone coming even close to its intended target, while Catch was already notching up frequent kills. One particular Saturday, I remember almost coming to grief when I discovered, just before setting off, that the pockets of my trousers were worn through and would carry no more ammunition. My mother's response to this crisis was to tell me 'If it covers your backside, 'twill do gallant.' Faced with the loss of a day's 'shooting', all stops were pulled out. Finally an old pea tin provided the answer. A hole bored through the top allowed a piece of baling twine to be looped through and I carried it slung over my shoulder. Not unlike how the Indians carried their arrows. It worked for many a day after.

In those days I learned the names of all the birds common in the locality. We learned to identify them not only by their size and colour, but also by their flight pattern and feeding habits. I quickly realized that I was something of a hero amongst my peers, not only for my ability to distinguish blackbirds from starlings by their markings, but even at great distances. How were they supposed to know that starlings were flocking birds, whereas blackbirds were more solitary. Even then, the intermittent hop of a blackbird was so different from the proud almost swaggering walk of the starling. Birds' nests, too, were distinguishable by size and shape and also by the materials used and the number, size and colour of eggs. Their songs of course we also knew, including their warning call whenever a prowling cat or other danger approached. Likewise, we could always spot the passes made through the hedges by rabbits, hares and foxes. All these things we learned to read like a separate language and even today this sense of what's happening in the countryside can add special satisfaction to a day's sport, be it fishing, shooting or just a happy walk. But although at this stage Catch was a sort of hero to me, it gradually became apparent that everything we did was inspired by a desire to impress Daddy. That big man, whose love for, and knowledge of, all country sports knew no bounds. The excitement of the hunt was always surpassed by retelling the story, trying always to impress, without ever telling a lie. This was one principle he taught us early and it has lived with us always, despite the kind of exaggerations we frequently hear.

Another trick, which he showed us, had the happy effect of teaching us a great truth. He spent quite a bit of time and no small amount of skill, not to mention patience, making a crib. This was something I've never yet seen anyone else do. At it's simplest it was a bird trap. A pyramid shaped cage, made of short lengths of hazel about finger thickness. Four uprights formed a frame and the sides were formed by ever shortening horizontals. This was designed to be set at an angle to the ground with a simple but effective tripping mechanism. Baited simply with roast potatoes or bread during times of hard weather, it was irresistible to all sorts of hungry birds. The rare beauty of this unlikely contraption, was that once trapped, the bird had the option of a free meal and could then be taken out gently by hand and released unharmed. The capture having been thus effected, did not require any kill for proof. Sometimes we would spend hours in some vantage point, watching and waiting to see some bird spring the trap, other times it was simply set and left while we went about our jobs. Several times we got lucky and caught two birds together and this provided great craic, for to claim a double it was necessary to take out each bird individually by hand and then release them.

Killing rats was another important function for us. Fortunately they never seemed to venture into the house, no doubt the plentiful supply of feedstuffs on the outside kept them happy and there was no shortage of hiding places as well. There were two clay banks on either side of the farmyard where they burrowed, within easy reach of where the hens received their daily rations. In those days we had no compunction about using gin traps; now very much out of favour. We usually wrapped some cloth round one of the jaws of the trap to avoid amputating a leg, which would then leave a wounded animal free. Those traps are now illegal and I would not mourn their loss, but in those days they certainly helped keep numbers in check.

At one particular time, things seemed to be getting out of hand, when both the rats and the jackdaws were taking over the hens' feeding trough. It was suddenly common-place to see up to half a dozen rats and a flock of hungry jackdaws vying for position and actually crowding out the hens. Fortunately for them, the hens seemed to have a special place in my Mother's heart.

Once she decided enough was enough, a plan was hatched, the simplicity of which was matched only by its effectiveness. Next day the door of the hen house remained firmly closed and as the time approached for feeding, the squawking of the hens grew so loud, I thought Daddy would lose patience and shoot them instead. When the food was put out the jackdaws appeared immediately and almost as quickly the rats came raiding. To this day I'm not sure if the old man fired just one shot or two from the old twenty gauge, but the silence which followed was as deafening as the racket which preceded it. Wide eyed with disbelief, I ran to do a tally and found he had shot two rats and no fewer than eight jackdaws. Within minutes the carnage had been cleared, the hens were back in control and Mammy, once again, was contentedly singing while she worked.

Happiness awaits.

CHAPTER TWO

The stone arched high into the sky and landed with a loud crack on the galvanized roof of the hayshed, grating it's way down along the irregular curve before falling vertically to the ground. Yes!, I said triumphantly, turning to Catch. That means I get to walk the ploughed field side. He agreed without fuss. We were going hunting and I had just won the right to pick the best side. I raced out through the little gate at the end of the house and vaulted the gate leading into the said field. It was early summer and the potatoes were in full blossom. Even as I crossed the gate I saw a flock of sparrows fly up into the hedge. In a hushed tone I told Catch where to expect a shot and we walked in unison, catapults at the ready. When I was still twenty yards away I got a clear view of one. I fired and missed. For my trouble I was told off for frightening them too soon. "Sorry", I said, but he was a perfect shot. "Take your time", he scolded. "Try to get close next time and you might actually hit something". I resolved to do better next time.

Suddenly, a blackbird perched on a briar ahead. I stayed quiet, stalking for all I was worth. Two more steps and I'll be close enough, I thought. He flew away. I cried out in anger. "Watch out", Catch called, "there's a flock of starlings coming over". As they passed we both fired together, the two stones shooting up through the flock just a yard apart. "We were close", I shouted, feeling proud that my shot was as good as his. I watched the stones falling and managed to pick up one. Always a lucky stone for me, second time round. I reloaded the catapult and we crossed the little garden and into the long field. Suddenly Catch shot a blackbird and I felt the familiar feeling of excitement and envy as we both struggled through the bushes to find it. Fondly we gazed at the lifeless bird and decided it was a cock. Even better.

We ran then and jumped the brook, several times, over and back, occasionally pelting stones at anything that caught our eye - buttercups, daisies, or whatever. Suddenly I remembered "The Virginian" had been on television the previous night. It was reckoned to be the best cowboy of the time but it was on too late and I wasn't allowed to stay up, so now Catch gave me a first hand account. As we walked on I savoured every gun fight, fist fight, and cattle round up that took place anywhere next or near Medicine Bow. We were back on track now, either side of the ditch, still talking happily, eyes peeled as always for a shot. When the rabbit bolted from a clump of rushes and ran for the cover of the ditch my one thought was to fire with full power. He was crossing me at about fifteen yards. I pulled for all I was worth and fired. The stone was bigger than average and I heard the crunch as it collided with his head. Head over heels he tumbled, twice, his momentum carrying him forward, landing on his back at the edge of a bunch of nettles.

I stood rooted to the spot, suddenly unable to think. His hind legs were kicking frantically. Christ! I thought, if he manages to roll over one kick will get him into the drain and away. I dropped the catapult then and ran, diving on top of him. I got several stings on my hands but nothing mattered except catching him and getting back from the ditch. "I shot him", I finally croaked. "Did you hit something?", Catch asked. By his tone I knew he didn't believe me. "I shot a rabbit", I shouted. The excitement in my voice brought Catch crashing through the ditch, pushing nettles and weeds aside. Disbelief turned to joy on his face when he saw the kill. I pointed then to the spot from where he had flushed, my hand tracing the line he had run, pausing at my feet to show where I had hit him, and finally the very spot where he fell. I was breathless as I held the now lifeless animal aloft. Suddenly, Catch asked where I fired from and for one terrible moment I wasn't sure. I spotted the catapult then, lying where I had dropped it. I raced to pick it up and now was able to show exactly how it happened. Again my hand pointed to the clump of rushes, followed the line to where Catch stood, and on to the edge of the nettles. The only detail I needed to explain was the speed he was running at. He took the rabbit to admire it as I reloaded and tried to hit the rush, just to show it was no fluke. I missed, but it didn't matter.

It was some time before we decided to carry on. We had no bag or even string so I had to carry him tucked under my arm, the catapult as always at the ready. Soon the effort of keeping it pressed against my body became too much so I changed sides. The relief however was short lived, the other arm tiring as quickly as the first. In the end I decided to carry him by the legs, leaving the catapult trailing from my right hand. It didn't matter now. I could not concentrate on watching the ditch. My eyes kept looking down at my prize. Holding him by the forelegs, his head arched backwards, sightless eyes staring almost accusingly at me. But all I could feel was pride and a kind of restless excitement, wanting to go home.

When we finally reached the "boreen" and tripped along the rutted path that led to the farmyard, I prayed silently that Daddy would be home. Suddenly I saw the familiar blue Anglia arriving at the front of the house. I raced the last fifty yards and scrambled over the gate and was standing at the car door waiting for Daddy to get out. He was a big man, tall, broad shouldered and very overweight. As he pulled himself out of the seat and stood up with the help of the car door, a huge grin spread over his big gentle face as he struggled to straighten the hat, which almost fell from his head. I saw the look on his face when he saw the rabbit but before I could speak, Catch was beside me and telling the story, clearly showing all the excitement I was manfully, though unsuccessfully, trying to hide.

Daddy took the rabbit, his huge hand dwarfing it 'till it almost disappeared. "We'll have stew tomorrow", was his only comment as he headed towards the pump, calling to me as he went, "bring a knife and a bucket". I rushed to comply, knowing that the compliment of having this thing skinned and prepared for tomorrow's dinner was the greatest praise I could have wished for. I raced inside and came out with a knife and bucket as requested and without further ado, Daddy set about skinning and cleaning the rabbit. I watched wide-eyed as he slit its stomach full length and pulled out its insides. Then the head and legs were removed and the skin was pulled down over its back and finally cut away at the rump. I filled the bucket with cold water and watched agog as it turned bright red when he placed the carcass inside. He washed it quickly and then emptied the contents out on the ground, momentarily turning the grass red.

He refilled the bucket and this time I noticed the colour wasn't so bright. Then he wrapped the cleanings in the discarded skin and told me to bury it in the dung heap at the end of the cowshed. There of course it would rot quickly and be spread as fertilizer. The bucket, with its precious load, was stood inside the kitchen door and left ready for the pot. All this time, Catch and myself were still talking excitedly and Daddy listened patiently, with only the occasional prompt to keep us going.

Later we did the milking and then went to Ballybryan to play football but my mind was on other things. That night, my sleep was disturbed by a playful, laughing rabbit who, time and again, bounded from my arms and gleefully danced his way to the safety of his burrow. It was late when I awoke next morning to find that Catch and Daddy had already gone, I know not where. At first, my two sisters were an appreciative audience, but they soon lost interest. So I decided to strike off on my own. After several hours and countless attempts I killed a sparrow. The sheer pride at having notched up two kills back to back is something I will never forget. I was, so to speak, on a roll.

Ballybrittan Bridge, on the Grand Canal near Rhode in Co. Offaly.

CHAPTER THREE

Daddy was forty-eight years old when I was born. Not bad considering that I have a little sister. In the twenty-two years of his life that remained, he did enough living to convince me that he was one of the greatest men that ever lived. He was a big man, broad shouldered and powerfully built. Stout was the word we would have used to describe the fact that he was very overweight. For all his strength, he was as gentle as a lamb. The big beaming smile was never far from his face. His hair, once ginger, then silvery white, was always covered when outdoors. His fine felt hat always seemed to appear on his head just as he passed through the doorway. For us to see him bareheaded outside, or wearing the hat inside would have signified that something was amiss. He was both good-humoured and good-natured, but it was his legendary lack of patience which endeared him to all who knew him. From a gust of wind that threatened to blow the hat from his head, all the way to a storm that might take the roof off the hayshed, or anything in between, his response was always the same. A string of curses and abuse that would set fire to a snowman. Then in an instant the smile would return to his face and the problem, whatever it might be, was dealt with.

All friends and neighbours knew this and some of them took great delight in testing his patience. One occasion that will live long in my memory was when we had a sow that needed ringing. This was a job that really required the use of a crush of some sort. Without such a luxury Daddy called on the help of a couple of willing neighbours, who along with Catch and Kevin were asked to hold the unfortunate pig. Patsy

McGovern, always one with an impish sense of humour, winked slyly at Mick Rigney and proceeded to make valiant attempts to catch the frightened animal. Time and again they lunged and missed and ended up chasing it round the stable and all but falling over each other in the process. Daddy's patience was never likely to live with this and it wasn't long before the air was turned blue with obscenities and he himself entered the fray. "Come out of the way" he roared as he cornered the pig and straddled it with one leg either side and grabbed it with his left hand under its lower jaw. "Give me here that ringers" he growled impatiently. The pig's front legs were clear of the ground and despite its massive struggling it could not wriggle free of his vice-like grip. Then, as we literally shook with merriment, he did the job himself. To ring a pig single-handed is no mean feat and one I've never seen any one else do, but he took it all in his stride and promptly forgot about it. He was an honest man and expected all those around him to behave in similar fashion, although he had no difficulty with applying his own set of rules to shooting.

I think this was common to many men of his time. For example, shooting hen pheasants was, and still is, strictly forbidden. To this day I don't completely agree with that rule, though I do observe it. Daddy always reckoned a hen tasted better and seemed to take genuinely more pleasure from shooting them. Lands which were preserved were another bugbear for him, though I suspect this had something to do with the fact that the preserves near where we lived were those of large landowners, and it was always nice to steal a march there. Since he was overweight and slow to move, this gave rise to a form of poaching which contravened another law. That is, shooting through the car window at birds on the ground. To be fair to him, I never saw him shoot anything on the ground where he had the option to let it fly. I can still feel the excitement of going for a drive with him, to those special places. Places where we could always expect a quick shot, driving slowly with the window down, eyes peeled for a bird, or indeed a landowner, then stopping the car, switching off the engine because even the vibration from a car engine ticking over was enough to cause a miss. There was always then the mad scramble by yours truly, out over the hedge or ditch, to grab the bird and be gone. Rightly or wrongly we always believed the penalty for being caught was the automatic loss of the game licence. To us this was serious business. Many of the places where we were welcome to shoot were bordering these very preserves and quite naturally this gave us easy access to simply nip over the border and do the business and be gone in a hurry. Thinking about it now it all sounds a bit harmless but there is no doubt that a bird so poached was always sweeter to the memory.

To add to the thrill, the local Guard, himself a serious shooting man, preserved what land he could for himself and was always on the lookout for miscreants like us. There never seemed much chance of a sympathetic hearing from him in the event of a complaint being made. To him, any gun removed from the parish would simply improve his chances. There was one particular occasion, which still lingers in the memory, on a beautiful frosty Sunday morning as we were walking up a laneway towards the car. Catch was then about fourteen and already carrying a gun borrowed from our brother-in-law, for which he was clearly too young to have a licence. He also had two hen pheasants in the bag and we were walking slowly with Daddy without a care in the world. Suddenly, through the hedge to our right we saw a man in uniform approaching. In an instant, Catch dived through the bushes on his left and crawled down into the drain, scratching himself badly as he went. Daddy and myself walked on nonchalantly hoping he had not been seen. Moments later, we realised it was only the local postman working on Sunday because it was so close to Christmas. En route he had decided to walk down the field to herd his few cattle. When he met us he stopped for a chat and when he saw Catch emerging from the drain he passed a few choice comments about the aforementioned Guard. As far as I recall, he had himself been spoken to a couple of times for being a little unsteady on the bike coming home from the village late at night so there was no love lost there. Come to think of it, some things have not changed much in the intervening years.

That incident gave us a fright but really did little to change our ways. Daddy was getting on in years and it seemed natural to him to let Catch do the running whenever the dog set at a distance. Even at that young age Catch was proving to be something of a crack shot and he was altogether too keen to wait 'till he was sixteen. He had then, and still has, great respect for a shotgun and knew only too well the damage it could do. I, of course, was only about nine and still quite contented to trudge along with the old man and throw stones at anything that moved with a catapult. "Grouse", the black and white Llewllyn was showing no signs of aging at that stage although I think he would have been about eight years old then. If he had ever been trained, he would certainly have been a fabulous dog. His work-rate and intuition were second to none and he had a wonderful nose. His only real failing was obedience. Or rather his total lack of it. As a pup he had been freely encouraged to chase hares and rabbits so it is unfair to blame him for being "wild". Training a dog was a concept which totally escaped Daddy. Actually, I myself many years later, broke new ground for the family when I attempted to crack that particular chestnut. I can modestly say that I had some measure of success. That's a story for another day, but I know now that it was just as well that Daddy never tried it. His patience just would not stand it.

Looking back, shooting over Grouse was at once both an exciting and frustrating game. From the moment he was released, either from a makeshift lead or the boot of the car, he simply did whatever he wished and anyone who wanted to shoot had to play his way. He covered ground like a low-flying aircraft and for the most part it was difficult to tell which field he was in. Usually he could be spotted at full speed passing a gap in a hedge, anything up to three fields away only to disappear again and reappear in a different field altogether. Once he stayed out of sight for an extra few minutes the race was on to find him for we knew he was likely to be set. He was, as they say, rock steady and the "Devil or Doctor Foster" wouldn't move him till we got there and actually pushed him forward to flush the bird.

Kevin, my eldest brother, while taking a certain interest in shooting was never as keen as Catch and myself although he really had a penchant for fishing or setting traps, cribs, snares or whatever. He seemed to have that instinctive touch that resulted in a kill more consistently. By this time however he had gone to England to make his fortune so most of my memories are of Catch and Daddy. About this time we acquired, by somewhat dubious means, a pellet gun. This was the greatest boon to our hunting so far and the rate of kills went up dramatically. We never actually had a licence for it so there was always that element of danger. But we managed to carry it far and wide without ever encountering the local sheriff. That weapon gave us more hours of pleasure than I would ever be able to recount though there were some stories that I will tell by and by. Now that the statute of limitations has passed !!. This thing could shoot all small birds, including blackbirds and thrushes, and I remember clearly one morning, Catch going out before school and accounting for no fewer than seventeen birds, mainly sparrows and redpoles. At the time we called them "Pee Wits" simply because of their call. The gun could also cater for rats and this gave it a certain legitimacy, so many a quiet hour was whiled away sitting on top of the hayrick or at some other vantage point, picking them off as they appeared near the hens' feed.

The Grand Canal, that noble waterway.

CHAPTER FOUR

Fishing was another sport for which I developed a great love. This was rather surprising because, although Daddy was fond of trout, he had not really got the patience to sit and watch a line though he did have his own unique method of capturing them. April and May are the months I remember as the times when, as he would say, "There's a certain softness in the air" and then the jar of worms were dug; blackheads we called them though they are more properly called blueheads. He was never without a ready supply of "night lines", usually up to a dozen which he would make in the night time; a short stick of ash or hazel with about ten or twelve yards of line tied on. The sinker consisted of a nut or washer and a hook whipped to gut. He never seemed to like the type with the eye for some reason.

Driving to the river was excitement personified and walking the bank till he found a likely looking spot and then setting the lines just far enough apart so they could not tangle. All this was done in the fading light of evening, ever watchful lest someone was in the vicinity. Partly because we might be reported and partly, because they might decide to check them before us in the morning. We would then retrace our steps along the dewey bank in the early summer's morning, looking for the little markers, sometimes a fencepost or bush or just simply a heelmark in the soft earth for which Daddy was amply built. Then lying flat on our bellies to feel along the water's edge to find the line and the excitement of feeling the feeble tug of a tired fish; that moment of dire tension as the trout was lifted over the edge and well back from the water. Suddenly the little

Hessian bag would appear in Daddy's hand for the prize and another worm was placed on the hook and the simple little trap cast back. From a dozen or so setlines, we would frequently pick up six or seven trout; usually about half to three-quarters of a pound in weight. The abiding memory I have of all this is the sight of those freshly caught fish curling upwards in the pan, their pink flesh calling for salt and the fresh homemade brown bread waiting on the table.

Throughout the summer we fished, that is to say legally with rod and line, on that great stretch of water known as the Grand Canal. This man-made piece of heaven was about a mile from where we lived and there, as the years went by, we learned to fish and swim. I smile now as I recall the times I was told "if you get drowned, don't come back here". It was deep, about six feet at the middle, and sadly over the years claimed it's fair share of lives though none in our area, thankfully. My first visit there was one of those experiences that will stay with me forever; a beautiful sunny day which at the time I convinced myself was the best possible for fishing. I was well tutored before ever we reached the bank about staying well back from the edge on pain of never being brought again. We had two rods, a beautiful three-piece cane belonging to Daddy, complete with reel and the second, a bamboo with the line attached to the top and wound around it when not in use. The function of the cork was well described to me in advance. This, I was told, was what fishing was all about, just waiting and watching to see it bob about in the water to signify a bite.

Catch set up and cast in my rod first and while he was busy getting the other one organised, I watched the cork floating happily on the mirror smooth surface.

Suddenly it sank and circled some four inches below the surface and it took a few seconds to force myself to shout. Catch, with all the ease in the world, simply dropped the rod he was holding and in one swift movement swung the other high over our heads and one very surprised bream was suddenly lying on the grass. All silvery and glisteny in the sun, his mouth opening and closing in a vain attempt to understand what had happened. We just knew this was our day and all that remained to be done was to "clean" the canal. It transpired that was our only take of the day. In those days we knew little of the finer points of fishing and we had no idea how to kill a fish. Consequently he was left gasping for oxygen until he eventually died. It was many years later that we learned how to use a "priest". From that day on, fishing became one of the great loves of my life. Catch, while he still enjoys it, was never really hooked and still rates shooting as the real sport.

As the years passed I was allowed to go fishing with pals my own age although always with the stern warning to stay well clear of the water's edge. One particular day I fished with a friend called Seamus Conroy. Oddly enough it was probably the only time in his life that he ever bothered to go. It was again a beautiful hot Sunday afternoon and we got lucky. That is to say, that with only my rod we managed to land no fewer than twenty-one fish, mostly perch, all fingerlings except for two which were of reasonable size. The fun really began when it was time to go home. We were not equipped with any sort of bag. I was dressed in my Sunday best, a suit consisting of coat and short pants. Without much ado, I removed the coat and tied knots at the end of each sleeve, wrapping the entire catch in the body of the coat. All this, I might add, was done to avoid dirtying the pockets. The innocence of youth!

On the long trip home the argument was over who would get to keep the two prize fish, a matter of little consequence since the entire lot was fed to the cat. We never ate the fish from the canal, as the water was too still and dirty. This probably accounts for the fact that there was never any attempt at poaching there. Now, more than thirty years later, though I regularly fish beautiful rivers and occasionally lakes, whenever I want to remember what it was like to be a small boy I see in my mind's eye, that noble waterway-The Grand Canal. Hard lessons learned there have stayed with me all my life.

Probably the best lesson learned was always to bring a plentiful supply of hooks. I still feel pangs of great sadness when I recall the days that were lost because my only hook got lost or I ran short of worms or whatever. My motto now is to always travel well prepared. There, too, I learned the joy of hunting for bigger fish. Spinning for pike was soon to become my main pleasure and although the average size of pike, at least those I caught, was about three to four pounds, their overall appearance made me feel they were the king of all fish. Nowadays I get a very similar feeling when fishing for salmon.

CHAPTER FIVE

When the summer holidays were over and the nights began drawing in, young boys, then as probably now, began to look to Halloween as the only excitement before Christmas. This was partly true in my case because although I enjoyed all the devilment which we got up to on the night, it held for me a much greater significance. This heralded the start of the shooting season on November 1st. That date is forever etched on my memory as the early winter frost made the beet tops crackle around our knees while the big Llewllyn Setter ranged freely and I trudged patiently behind Daddy and Patsy McGovern, with Catch increasingly taking over from the big man in carrying the gun. That sudden buzz of excitement whenever the dog set, as the men rushed to take position while I moved behind the dog to coax him forward. Time suddenly standing still, complete silence, guns at the ready as each man tried to gauge where the bird would flush.

Earlier agreements about who gets first shot are suddenly forgotten as the tension mounts. The pressure to bring home feathers on the first day adds to the moment, and as the dog crawls forward and changes direction I notice movement all around as the guns adjust their positions. When suddenly a young cock flushes I wait wide eyed as the race to cover him and fire the first shot is on. Suddenly two shots sound, too close to decide later who was first but the cock falls close to the ditch with a broken wing and then there is another race to catch him before he reaches cover. That was a race usually won by the dog though not always. Daddy had a long held belief that a hungry dog hunted better and so it was usual not to feed him the previous day. I recall one occasion when the dog caught a runner on the other side of a river and promptly sat and devoured it. The old man came as close to breaking then as I've ever seen and twice aimed the gun to shoot but somehow managed to refrain. The poor dog was in the bad books for a long while after that.

Hen pheasants were shot without consideration in those days and Daddy always claimed that they tasted sweeter. Furthermore he felt that as the season progressed, it was frustrating for a dog to set and flush hens consistently and watch them fly away unhindered. That was something our "Grouse" did not suffer too often. On more than one occasion I saw Patsy McGovern allow a hen to escape and when the old man tried to rebuke him he would simply say with a grin "she was the wrong colour". By the time he was fourteen, Catch was doing most of the shooting, partly because Daddy was slowing down but also because the old man actually enjoyed letting him shoot.

He was a damn good shot who also had the inherent instincts of a poacher. His speciality was to shoot the very edges of the big preserves and allow the dog to range far into enemy territory and wait for a set. Then with a quick glance round, he would clear the ditch and run in a crouch, shoot anything that got up, whatever it's colour and be gone in the blink of an eye. On more than one occasion he was chased but by men much older than himself who could not even get close enough to identify him, let alone catch him. Edgel's, Thong's, Cotton's and Neal's were the main farms which were "strictly preserved", and also there were one or two contrary individuals who, though they didn't own enough land to be worth preserving, they would sometimes get awkward about letting anyone cross the ground. Added to all that was the fact that the local Guard erected signs at strategic places and this further reduced our free travel. All in all the countryside to us looked something like a patchwork quilt with different colours showing the areas where we were or were not welcome.

It was about this time that I began to understand the wisdom of the old man's habit of "giving a bird". This practice had me somewhat stumped for a time, because he had a real love for game. But as I travelled frequently with him to various houses to deliver a bird I would hear the genuine gratitude in peoples' voices and began to realize how well this simple offering kept us on good terms. This was especially evident when he told his frequent stories about how this or that bird had been "poached" from some of the aforementioned "preserves". Nowadays, while shooting over land where I don't always know the farmer personally, I find that whenever I meet them in the field, an offer of an occasional bird can really generate a welcome.

Tommy Walton, left of picture, with his son Gregg and the author

CHAPTER SIX

The pheasant shooting, then as now, only lasted for three months of the year but Catch and myself were keeping our hand in, so to speak, the whole year round with the various other means which we had at out disposal. Although we were, and still are by our nature very careful with any kind of gun, there were times when youthful exuberance caused us to think we were invincible and act accordingly. One such time is a story never before told and I guess now is as good a time as any. Catch was using the pellet gun with the kind of precision which was common among the cowboys on the telly and during idle times in the old cowshed he would amuse himself, and me, by shooting tiny objects such as very small potatoes at a range of maybe twelve feet. Then one day we were playing cowboys, and as I stood at a corner waiting for him to appear, he came up behind me and decided to shoot the little red star which was protruding from my holster. The sudden sound of the shot, coupled with the sound of the plastic breaking, made me jump but when I saw the damage done to my beautiful holster I wanted to cry. When I finally realized the quality of the shot the damage was soon forgotten. We knew now was the time for some real challenge.

Suddenly I was put standing with a small spud, about the size of a large marble, on top of my head and told to stand very still while he rested the gun on the concrete manger and I felt the spud explode with the force of the pellet. Now we had a real game, but one which two could play because although he was the one doing the shooting, I had to play a vital part by standing perfectly still since any movement would destroy even the best shot. Soon I graduated to tilting my head right back and balancing the potato between my upper lip and my nose. This was even better because he had to be really quick as it was more difficult to hold my head in that position for more than a few seconds. I have no idea how many times we did that, but as I still have all my vital organs I can verify that we were always lucky. Then one day, things took a rather dramatic turn.

We were in the calf-house waiting for a chance of a shot at a swallow or maybe a willie wag on the dung-heap outside. Suddenly, the peace was shattered by the loud cackling of one of Mother's prize hens telling the world in general that another egg had appeared. She had laid in the corner of the old makeshift wooden manger and now stood proudly with feathers fluffed out making a racket we could see no need for. From where he was standing, Catch pointed the gun in her direction and said almost casually, "I wonder if I put a pellet through her tail now, would you see the hole when her feathers settle down". Without much further thought the experiment was deemed worthwhile and he nonchalantly squeezed the trigger. With a painful, frightened, squawk the bird suddenly lurched to one side, her right leg shattered and she somehow managed to avoid falling off her perch. The silence which descended was deafening in its totality. In Catch's face, I could see a mirror of the desperate panic which was welling up inside myself. Any blood he had was in his toes.

Probably ten seconds passed before any movement was made. Then he went to the opening in the front of the shed, which served as a window and surveyed the farmyard to be sure no one was close enough to know what had happened. A hasty meeting was convened, at which he was Chairman, main speaker and final arbitrator all in one. It was quite obvious that to inform Mother about this would result in a sudden demand for all out decommissioning of weapons. In modern parlance, we were not yet in decommissioning mindset so a plan was quickly hatched. The hen had to go. There was simply no other way. In one swift movement he plucked the still startled hen from her lobsided perch and, without further ado, rang her neck. There was an old door lying idle against the wall which had not been stirred for donkeys years and it was behind this that the "corpse" was hastily hidden under some straw, to be disposed of later under cover of darkness so to speak.

As luck would have it that was the week of the Womens' Mission in the Parish and we knew that as soon as the tea was over, Daddy would drive any women within range to the village church and drink a couple of bottles of stout while their souls were being saved. Who could ever doubt the value of religion after that? Once the plan was hatched we knew that the best way to avoid detection was to stay well away from that shed. For the rest of the day the minutes dragged like hours as we tried at all costs to stay clear of the shed, yet stay close enough to see that no one else went in there. When it finally came time to bring the cows in for milking we were off in a canter, knowing that all was going our way and that the rush to finish the milking and prepare the tea would leave no time for anyone to go near the crime scene. The Mission took priority over all else, so that even as we took the cows back out to pasture for the night, the women were already in various stages of preparation. It was with great delight that we, that is Catch and I, were last to sit down to our supper.

Suddenly Daddy appeared in the kitchen putting the final touches to his hair and lifting the famous hat and telling one and all that it was time to be going. There was the usual searching of handbags, looking for Rosary Beads and small change for the box and suddenly they were all in the car. Daddy, Mammy, Aunt Mary and our two sisters Nuala and Fran. As the car left the front yard we walked aimlessly to the road to watch it out of sight. Then we did a final run through the entire house just to check that there were no stray females lurking in the shadows. With almost military precision we left through the back door and I took up position at the gable end of the house, from where I could hear if the car should return and at the same time be able to signal to Catch that the coast was clear.

He entered the calf-house through the window and almost immediately his head reappeared looking anxiously for a signal. One wave of my arm and he was out and running for the gap which led to the brook field, with the Rhode Island Red tucked, as best he could, under his half coat. As soon as he was out of the yard, I was following his footsteps as fast as my ten-year-old legs would allow. Away we went to the farthest corner of the field, to an old ivy tree where we had already agreed that we would dispose of that awesome burden. With only a single glance back to the house, he dropped the bird and started to climb. Moments later his feet were lost in the mass of ivy and for one terrible moment I felt like I was all alone. Then the leaves parted near the top and his hands and face peered through as he called for me to throw him the hen. At the first attempt I missed by a country mile and for a moment I thought it was going to snag on a branch and remain there for the whole world to see. Luckily it fell back to earth and at the second time of asking I put it right in his hand. That was the last I ever saw of it.

We went back then to check that all feathers, and any other evidence, were cleaned up in the calf-house and I know it was a long time before we even ventured near that tree again. That incident, as much as any other that ever happened between us, formed a bond which all the trials of the intervening thirty odd years have failed to break. At the time, we could have imagined no more serious secret which we might ever have to keep and I tell it now only in the happy knowledge that it doesn't matter any more. Fortunately, it also taught us a very valuable lesson. That misplaced shot, which so suddenly crippled the chicken, could so easily have taken the eye out of my head. For many days after, we came up with all sorts of explanations as to why the shot went wrong. A distraction, or a faulty pellet, or maybe the chicken was even stupid enough to move at the wrong time but whatever way we looked at it our game of trick shooting was over for all time.

CHAPTER SEVEN

While on the subject of that pellet gun, and all the memories it evokes, there are two shots which stand out in my mind though it is now more than thirty years ago. One was a shot which I took myself and the other which was taken by Catch, had remarkably similar consequences. As I have tried to explain, we learned early on to have a great love and respect for the game, which we hunted. This, however, was not quite enough to stop me doing something which I regretted for many a long day. The incident happened in early summer and I can vividly recall the beautiful sunny weather.

I had been having something of a lean time although all around me I could hear the frustrating sounds of all those songbirds thrilling for the sheer joy of living. As usual we had spent many hours searching for birds' nests and there was one which really got to me. A thrush had made her annual home in the ivy at the top of an old ash tree, which was as near as we ever came to having a tree house. High up among the dense foliage I would often sit for hours whenever I wanted to be alone. The peace up there was special to me.

Now, however, I had to stay away and allow the chicks to hatch. We had of course counted the eggs a couple of times and were keeping a discreet eye on the proceedings. Many times through the day I would stalk quietly to the bottom of the tree and watch the mother bird sitting brooding. Only her head and tail were visible. The frustration of not getting a shot, coupled with having to vacate my special place in the tree, was getting to me. At first, I merely drew a bead on the nest for the want of something better to do. Knowing of course that to shoot a bird on the nest was unthinkable.

After I had done that a few times I began to convince myself that I would be very unlikely to hit her. Again I approached the tree and as I looked up she was watching me squarely. Once again I took aim, this time specifically at her eye. Who would ever score such a hit? For a long time I held my aim. The warm sun was burning the back of my neck and making my palms sweaty. Then almost without deciding, I squeezed the trigger. The pellet hit her in the eye. Her death was as sudden as it is possible to imagine. I knew how wrong I was. I walked away, for fear anyone should see me, and spent a few minutes thinking. I decided to remove the corpse and pretend to Catch that she had forsaken the nest for some reason.

My heart was as heavy as I had ever known as I climbed that tree and removed her. I started to think about where I would hide the evidence, but knew almost at once that this was one lie I could not tell. After a long wait, Catch came home and I took him to the cowshed to tell all. I expected to be in a lot of trouble for I knew how disappointed he would be. However, he seemed to sense my guilt and realised that I needed no further punishment. Then he even tried to console me with the thought that any bird which I might shoot at that time was likely to have a nest full of young at home. This really did little to make me feel better and the thought of the sheer wasteful cruelty of the deed stayed with me for years after.

By a strange coincidence something similar happened to Catch some time later, which he told me about in passing, many years hence. He was shooting, again on a lovely summer's evening, not far from an old graveyard in Ballymacwilliam when he spotted a hare sitting some ten yards out from a ditch. He had to stalk for about a hundred yards along the inside of the ditch until he came to a point opposite the target. He steadied himself and waited for his breathing to settle before drawing a bead and aimed purposefully for the animal's eye. Again the pellet found its mark. This time, though, death was far from instant. He can remember the dull thud as the lead struck. The hare pitched sideways with the most pitiful scream imaginable. Then, in blind terror, he began to roll and jump in wide circles. Catch dropped the gun and scrambled through the ditch to put the poor thing out of its misery. But the animal's movements were so erratic that it took several minutes to catch it while all the time he could hear the tortured screams.

Finally, he caught it and dispatched it cleanly with a chop to the back of the neck. He, too, was badly shaken by the incident and only ever talked about it after a time had elapsed. Some people would describe all hunters as cruel, but we would argue that we never would inflict needless pain on any creature. To kill something cleanly was always the aim and bore no relation to the kind of mindless thuggery which is all too prevalent in suburban life today. How people can casually inflict the kind of injuries we so often hear about on living creatures is really beyond me.

CHAPTER EIGHT

This is not the kind of book where one would expect to find Ghost stories. Nonetheless, one story which has always stood out in my mind could be put in that category. As far as I can remember, I would have been about ten years old at the time. It was mid December and the pheasants were getting scarce. An individual, who shall remain nameless, was playing havoc with all of Catch's best attempts to relieve him of some of his precious birds. He seemed to know the times when we were likely to be prowling, and even changing our timetable seemed to be of no benefit.

Whatever time we came along, he always seemed to be wandering around the field for no apparent reason. Actually, he only owned about two fields in total. But it was prime feeding for game and the only real hunting ground in the area. There was an ash and oak wood of about two acres next to his land where the pheasants roosted at dusk and all else around was bare green fields. We knew that there were at least a couple of cocks in the place and maybe more. Catch devised a plan, which was brilliant in its simplicity. Dawn was deemed to be the time when we were most likely to catch him napping, so to speak. Daddy, as ever, was only too willing to drop us at the Canal Bridge well before daylight. The walk along the canal bank took us directly past his front door. We knew he didn't have a dog so we were confident enough as we strode quietly by.

Grouse was on a leash and my part in the game was to wait in the boundary drain, holding the dog, while Catch went to take cover near the edge of the wood, which was at the bottom of the long field of stubbles. Before he left, he tied the dog's leash to a root in the bottom of the drain and warned me to stay down and out of sight. "When daylight breaks, you will hear a few shots and when I call you, release the dog and follow on". It was now about six forty- five, and the minutes dragged by. Of course he had the only watch, so all I could do was guess the time. There was a hard frost on the ground and the cold was severe after the first few minutes. The sky overhead was dark, with only a few stars showing. Behind me I could hear the water in the canal lapping and occasionally the sound of songbirds fluttering in the bushes startled me. After a while I climbed out of the drain to check that our enemy was not coming down the bank for an early morning stroll. The fear of being caught was really getting to me. I could visualize myself being hauled off to the Guards barracks and questioned about what I was doing so far from home at that unearthly hour and trying to think of an excuse which would not involve Catch.

Gradually the sky began to brighten and I could begin to make out my surroundings. I could peer gradually further down the field and then the shape of the wood began to emerge. The dawn chorus was getting louder although at that time I did not know what it was called. Again I went to check if the old man was coming, and breathed a sigh of relief to find that all was quiet on the bank. Grouse was straining at the leash, which was only a makeshift made from rope and I was patting him to keep him quiet. Still there was no sound of any shots. I knew that Catch intended to shoot anything that moved, whatever it's colour, and was hoping that once the sound of the shot had gone things would settle down and the rest of the birds would come out as normal. The bottom of the field was getting clearer now and I hoped and prayed that something would happen soon because I was cold and really quite frightened. Anxiously, I scanned the far end of the field and then again I went to check the canal bank. All was well. Once more I climbed down into the drain and patted the dog, all the time talking to him to take my mind off my predicament. It was then I saw him.

He was standing in the farthest corner of the field, right where I expected him to be. Catch, with the gun in his left hand, was waving at me furiously to release the dog. Obviously, I thought the birds had all decided to feed in some other field at the far side of the wood this morning, and it was time to be after them. I untied the dog and he was away in a flash, stopping briefly midway down the field to relieve himself. I scrambled out of the drain and suddenly realised the leash was still tied to the root so I hurried back and fumbled to untie it. I ran flat out down the middle of the field, knowing that Catch would not be pleased if I delayed, and anyway I wanted to be as far away from that man's house as possible.

The scene which greeted me at the other end of the field is one I will never forget. Catch was standing facing the wood trying desperately to draw a bead on any one of the many birds that were flying in all directions. The crowing of cocks was deafening. Suddenly, he turned to me and asked how the hell did the dog manage to get loose. Struggling for breath, I told him, "I let him go as soon as you called me. Who called you?," he almost roared at me. "I saw you standing there and waving for me to come", I protested. The dog was in the wood now and running wild. Still more cocks were crowing and Catch was getting madder by the minute. If I had a witness to the names he called me, I could probably take a case against him even now. As we struggled through the wood and began the long walk home, all I could hear was a torrent of abuse. No amount of explaining was sufficient to make him see my side of the story. I am not sure why the plan was not deemed to be worth another try, on another day. Suffice to say that for years after, I was blamed for ruining what could have been his best ever day's shooting.

As I write, it is almost thirty-five years since that incident. Still, in my mind's eye, I can see him, wearing an old suede jacket with a white fur collar, not exactly ideal camouflage gear, standing and waving at me. How the mind can play tricks!. The story took on a new significance in the mid-eighties when, as a bus driver, I had to drive a coach load of pilgrims to pray and marvel at the wonders of a moving statue near Ballinspittle, Co. Cork. As luck would have it, it was on the first Saturday night in September and I had spent the day on the mountain hunting grouse after a very late night on Friday. Three-and-a-half hours listening to rosaries, and hearing of the wonder of this phenomenon were just what I did not need. And that was just on the way there.

When we arrived in Ballinspittle I saw a statue, mounted high up on a hillside, illuminated by lights from at least three different directions. The background consisted of fir trees, which were waving in the breeze and, just to enhance the effect, the crowd, who were praying at the scene were continually flashing lights in all directions. How anyone could believe, in such circumstances, that they saw a hand move or teardrops appear is beyond me. At least, I consoled myself, I was a lonely, frightened child at the time of my vision. What,

I wondered, would be their excuse, whenever they came back to reality.

Catch (left) and Tommy, to the mountains bound.

Grouse and Sally on their first trip to the mountain.

CHAPTER NINE

Looking back on a childhood that was basically happy, it can be difficult to tell in which particular year various events took place. One exception to this is the year of 1967. That was the year in which Catch became sixteen. No doubt, in that year many things happened to him, which are of no real importance here. Leaving school and taking up employment, not to mention playing some very good football, and possibly even chasing the odd girl. Possibly even one or two who were not so odd. But becoming sixteen had a great significance in our lives. That was the time when it became legal for him to carry a gun. Getting a licence was something of a double-edged sword. On the one hand, it meant being able to go where we liked without the fear of being reported. It also meant that, that which he had never held before could now be taken away. So I guess he did a spot of soul searching and decided that some of his old habits had to change. He reckoned that if he were going to risk being caught doing something illegal, then he would at least make it something "honourable". Suddenly the act of shooting birds on the ground became restricted to the strictest preserves, of which there were a few. Hen pheasants were a definite no-no. This unfortunately brought him into direct conflict with Daddy, in a way to which we were totally unaccustomed.

Familial rows were as much a part of our household as any other. They were usually sudden loud eruptions, when everyone had their say, and the issue was then forgotten. The shooting of hen pheasants became something of a battle of wills, between Catch and Daddy. Although I was only eleven, I could sense the tension which was mounting and knew I was powerless to do anything to help. On several occasions when Catch and I went shooting on our own, as we did frequently, I saw him allow the grey birds to fly unhindered. Then when we would arrive home, I was invariably told to stay quiet and leave the telling of the story to Catch. This he did by usually telling of hens which rose out of range or which were really too young to shoot. Daddy, being the wily old fox that he was, wasn't buying this for long and soon began to make remarks about the fact. He was more than fond of his meat and since he always felt that hen pheasants tasted sweeter, he was not about to keep quiet now. Then one day, all three of us were out together, with Catch carrying the twenty gauge, while Daddy had a twelve gauge, which was on loan from our brother-in-law, Sean Foy. When the dog set on the wrong side of the boundary Catch had no problems about crossing. A hen flushed and Catch decided to hold fire. I could see anger building in the old man and, when Catch returned, he exploded, saying that was a glorious chance to miss. Catch simply said that it wasn't worth the risk. At that stage Daddy said one of the few hurtful things he ever said. "Were you afraid or what"? There was no more said but I knew instinctively that the matter would not rest there.

The rest of the day passed without any further comment about the matter, but there was suddenly a strain between them, which I knew was not right. As the following weeks passed, I was filled with a sense of foreboding. I could feel the thunder in the air and knew that some time or other the cloudburst would come.

On a Friday night soon afterwards, we were talking about the season and the number of birds which we had and arranged to take a drive the following morning. At this stage we had a fair idea of where we would likely get a shot. The morning was winterish with a strong wind and squally showers falling intermittently. As we left home that morning, I was not fooled by the happy nature of the two men. Silently I prayed that we would meet only cocks and then we would have no problem. Catch was at a stage where rebellion was the order of the day and the old man was silently bemoaning the passing of the son, whom he had so carefully moulded.

The first half-hour went without incident and then we saw the first cock of the morning. He was picking, quite contentedly, in a field of stubbles belonging to Edgels. He was some two hundred yards from the road and ordinarily not worth bothering about. There was, however, a cock of straw in the field which for some reason had not been brought in at the harvest, which was now of no real use to anybody. Anybody except us that is, for by driving a further fifty yards along the road it offered the perfect cover.

They discussed the situation briefly. Catch decided that if he ran to the cock of straw quickly enough, there was a good chance that he would get a shot. It was early in the morning and there was little chance of either of the two Edgel brothers catching us. Catch was out of the car and running in the blink of an eye, and covered the distance to the cock of straw in a crouching sprint. Then he steadied himself and took a couple of deep breaths before showing himself to the cock. The poor bird did the only thing possible. He rose, crowing in panic and was shot cleanly with the first shot. Catch then did what he so often drilled into me to do, in the years to come. He reloaded the gun, ever mindful of the chance of a second shot. Then he darted forward, picked up the bird, and turned to race for the car.

The cock's tail was dragging along the ground from his left hand, while the gun in his right was pointing towards the sky. He was running back along pretty much the same track, which he had used on the outward journey and was taken totally by surprise when two hens flushed almost at his feet and flew in either direction. One to the left and the other to the right. What happened next is forever indelibly printed on my memory.

Catch stopped, dropped the bird he was carrying, and swung the gun to cover the bird to his left. The hen fell, as though from a heart-attack, and he had almost covered the second before I heard the sound of the shot. Similarly the second one fell silently and he was already moving to pick the cock at his feet when the second shot sounded. I was over the moon. The quality of the shooting was clear to be seen and I knew that Catch would want to talk about this for a long time to come. At the same time I knew that Daddy would be happy, so I thought it was one of those rare occasions where everybody got what they wanted.

Moments later, Catch was back in the car and we were driving away. The old man, who was much more conscious of the hurt which his previous remarks had caused, said simply. "I was surprised to see you shoot them". Catch dropped the three birds at his feet with a look on his face which I couldn't really understand and replied, "that's at least four clutches of young birds which will not be around next year, but at least I was not afraid to shoot them". There was a sting to his words and the next ten minutes passed in total silence. I wanted to congratulate him on the achievement, but sensed this was not the time. Then, Daddy broke the silence. "I suppose you are right. It is a shame when you think about it, to be shooting next year's breeding stock". In an instant, the tension seemed to drift from the car, like electricity being turned off and all was suddenly well in the camp again. I believe I can say, without fear of contradiction, that from that day forward, the shooting of hen pheasants became anathema to our family culture. When my turn came, as it did much later, to follow a gun, this was one crime of which I was never guilty. But in fairness, it must be said that the ground breaking was done by my big brother.

A camping trip with the boys. Coumshingaun, circa 1987.

CHAPTER TEN

The years that followed were happy, formative ones for me. My three older sisters all acquired boyfriends, who in turn became husbands, which amounted to brothers-in-law to me. These same individuals also had a keen interest in shooting. One of them, Pat Murphy, in fairness was never one to follow a gun himself, but rather was content to come along for the walk. Sean Foy and Pascal Kavanagh were both keen gun-men in their day although they both gave it up some time after they were married. To this day it is still a family joke that they only feigned interest to curry favour with "ould Johnny Grennan". Once the two daughters were safely won, the shooting stopped. Nonetheless, in the time that they did spend shooting with Catch and myself, great friendships were formed which have stood the test of time.

In those days, Sundays in winter all followed a similar pattern. First Mass at eight o'clock, followed by a quick breakfast and a short drive to where we could shoot handy and be home for dinner at about half past twelve. Then after a leisurely break, we would be gone again for the afternoon, rarely returning before dark. The number of farmers over whose lands we were welcome to shoot would be too extensive to list here. But suffice to say that now, some thirty years on, it is still a joy to go back and meet those same people and be told repeatedly that we are still welcome.

One of the great lessons of life which shooting taught me is the value of the half chance. This is true in all sports to a degree. One only needs to look at a game of hurling or football to appreciate the value of a forward who can create scores from nothing and the joy

47

of punishing defensive errors is what the game is all about. A feature of shooting, like so many other sports, is that accuracy and kill rates seem to peak with pressure. The more important the game, the greater the focus. The times when we ran, crouching to a set dog well inside the border of some of those famous preserves. Eyes scanning the surrounding fields for any sign of the owner, knowing that the sound of a shot would bring him running always heightened the thrill. Those were the times when you could not afford to miss. Then, there was the frantic scramble to pick the bird up and get away. Running then, till we were well out of range and breathless, occasionally hearing the strains of "If you don't come back, I'll kill you" ringing in our ears. A bird, so poached, always seemed to taste extra sweet.

At those times too, there was real danger as we ran full belt across open bog. Frequently, in the half-light of dusk we jumped over bog-holes, which were deep enough to drown in and almost impossible to escape from, even by a capable swimmer because of the steep sides. The temperature of the water, in mid winter, was nothing to look forward to. Fortunately, as with our earlier escapades with the pellet gun, luck seemed to be always on our side and we never suffered any real mishap.

Catch, however, has often told a story of being followed by a man who shall remain nameless and who seemed to be gaining ground on him rapidly when he came to a very wide deep drain with no way around it. Without pausing to think, he jumped and failed to make the last few inches. He scrambled out and continued to run with two wellingtons full of water and moments later heard a splash as his pursuer plunged headlong into the water.

For a moment, he stopped and contemplated going back to help although he was well aware of this man's temper. Then he saw him emerge, soaking wet and raging like a wounded bull. At that point he expected the chase to end, but suddenly the bitter old pill came on without even bothering to empty his boots. At that stage, Catch was in the rather awkward position of running away from the general direction of home and his tormentor was well aware of this. On his right was the Grand Canal, which cut off any hope of circling back so he was left with no option but to run straight ahead and try to make it to the next bridge. This, he eventually managed and evaded capture, only to find himself in even less welcoming territory with which he was not nearly so familiar. It was very late when he finally reached home. The family were thinking all sorts, knowing that a gun at the best of times is a dangerous weapon and also that he was hunting alongside the canal, which had claimed more than it's fair share of victims down through the years.

On other occasions, the shooting was not nearly so serious when we walked in various combinations of one, two, three, four or even five, depending on how many of the family were available and simply talked about all the things in life which excite young men. Football, girls and suchlike. At times when we would walk for hours without seeing a pheasant, or getting any sort of a reasonable shot I can remember all guns coming up spontaneously and firing at some small song bird or even on occasion just a peculiar branch of a tree, just to break the boredom. Then, laughingly, we would say that those cartridges were too long in the gun and were becoming unlucky.

One of the great joys of the game, then as now, was the feeling of coming home late in the evening, totally exhausted after trudging for hours through muddy, wet fields, legs aching from the effort of jumping drains and ditches and chasing game, looking forward to the comfort of home. The thoughts of a bath, clean clothes and hot food and then relaxing with a good book or a few pints in the local were enough to warm the cockles of your heart. So many times down through the years I have heard people who were anti field-sports querying how we derive pleasure from simply shooting defenceless birds. How little they know!

My son Shane with his young cousin Philip Foran on Sliabh na mBan summit

CHAPTER ELEVEN

As the years passed, we paid scant attention to the changes which were coming over Daddy. Oh, the folly of youth !. Much of his time was spent resting in bed now, content to listen to our tales when we returned from a hunt. The shine was still in his eyes and the excitement never diminished. For hours he would lie there and hear the stories that were really only reruns of what he had taught us. But time was moving on for all of us. I had now reached the ripe old age of sixteen and completed my formal education; a modest Group Cert. Now I wanted to travel the world. Australia and South Africa were calling loudly. Catch had already gone to London while Kevin, our eldest brother, had returned home. Suddenly the great desire to shoot pheasants was replaced by thoughts of the mighty safaris, which I would embark on in foreign lands. The logical first port of call was London where Catch was waiting. There, I intended to earn enough money with which to take on the world.

Arriving in the big smoke for the first time suddenly brings the term "culture shock" to mind. After the wide open spaces, the noise of twenty-four hour traffic took some getting used to. Tall buildings and flashing lights with lanes of traffic going hither, tither and yon, with everybody in a hurry was both exhilarating and frightening all at once. But here, too, was the chance to really start to live as I pleased; no one listening to hear me come in late or ask where I had been. Fun, freedom and a whole lifetime were stretching out before me.

That great city held every possible mix of human being. With Heathrow airport only an hour away on the tube, it also seemed like a great starting point for any adventure we wished for. Even still, school friends who never travelled tend to ask me about places like Piccadilly Circus and what sort of goings on we indulged in. But even here the chance to shoot was what caught our fancy. Well, most of the time anyway. That very heartland of wild London was to provide us with some unexpected reminders of home. We found an amusement arcade where we were to spend many hours at a machine that showed a picture so reminiscent of our youth. The scene was a beautiful duck pond with lots of cover and a little barking dog who, whenever we put our ten pence in the slot, would run barking into the water and flush ducks to our hearts' content while we fired from an electric shotgun.

How often we joked about what our old friends would say if they could see us enjoying such simple pleasures in what seemed like the pleasure capital of the world. In that same arcade was another stall where there was a chance to make some real money. For fifty pence a time, we could buy three bullets and try to shoot out a red figure three from a white card. This was for a jackpot, which was rising nightly as long as nobody managed to succeed. As far as I recall it stood at about sixty-five pounds. That, when you consider that we were working hard on building sites for about thirty five pounds a week, was real money. We tried several times, always coming close until finally we challenged the man on the stall to prove that it could be done. He then produced a card and an empty shell and proved conclusively that with pinpoint accuracy, it was possible.

At that stage we decided that as Catch was consistently closer than I, it was sensible to let him do all the shooting with me paying half the cost and splitting the winnings at the end. I do not recall how often we went there, or how much money we spent but we knew that he was close enough to warrant continuing. Then one night he cracked it. I remember a crowd had gathered to watch, for they knew we were serious. A huge roar went up when he fired the final shot and the attendant smiled gaily as he retrieved the card and said almost glibly, "that's a winner". He then called over his boss who he said was the man to pay out the money. Eagerly the crowd waited. They were well-wishers to a man.

Then the boss deftly took the card in his left hand and rather roughly pushed his right fore-finger through the hole from the rear, to reveal the merest trace of red. Almost invisible to the naked eye, yet, on the strength of that he refused to pay out. From the back of the crowd there came an angry call "play fair now, pay the woman or leave the bed", and for a few moments I really thought he was going to have a riot on his hands. However, he stuck to his guns, (no pun intended), and refused to pay. Thereafter we boycotted the stand and never tried again. For what it's worth, I still say we were diddled.

Some time after that I discovered, tucked away discreetly on a side street, a gun shop that could supply just about any make of gun imaginable. Here I purchased an air pistol, which could be bought in the U. K. without any licence and once again we were off getting ourselves into trouble. Many times with that weapon, we roamed through Hampstead Heath, one of the great wild parks in London, shooting small birds while trying to avoid being seen by any of the thousands of walkers who used those woods. That gun provided many hours of fun and some very memorable shots, not least of which was on an Autumn morning when we spent ages stalking a beautiful bird with which we were not familiar. That is to say, that it was not one we had ever seen at home. We had seen the birds in the park before but we had no idea what they were. It was bigger than a mistle-thrush with a beautiful blue flash on its wings. We could approach to about twenty yards but then each time it would fly to a new perch. Eventually I got a long shot at it high up on an ash tree and was pleased to see it fall. Just then, a woman came along from the other direction and the only thing for it was to disappear. Some time later we went back and spent a while searching around until we found it. Then we were able to get a good look at it for the first time and later identified it as a Jay.

There was another occasion, which I have good reason to recall. I had been visiting friends up the country on a Sunday with my newly acquired wife and on our return to London we decided to drop in to a late night drinking house, known as " The Kebab House" where we had dinner and got talking to some people we knew, the result being that we stayed rather late. Some time around midnight, I can recall seeing a uniformed police man come in and speak to the owner of the place. The owner approached me and asked if I was driving car reg. no. such-and-such, and when I confirmed that it was my car he assured me in broken English that there was no problem.

I offered to move the car and was again assured that it was fine. Fortunately, I was not drinking that night, but it was some time near four-thirty a.m when we eventually left to go home. The earlier incident had long been forgotten about. I recall getting to the point of putting the key in the car door and suddenly being surrounded by five burly men who quickly flashed warrant cards at me which identified them as Special Branch. At that moment I realised that the gun was clearly visible on the back seat and the gravity of the situation was not long in setting in when I realised just how many police man hours I had wasted. I was most profuse about apologising and, to be fair to our British neighbours, they saw the funny side of it and let me off with a caution. Even today, I sometimes think how lucky I was, given how many claims we have heard of wrongful arrest under the Prevention of Terrorism Act.

Not long after that incident with the police, I had occasion to take a day off work. Just why, I cannot remember. I was about to go out when the doorbell rang. As I raced down stairs there was not a sad thought in my head. I opened the door to see a young lad who stuffed a telegram into my hand. I cannot recall if he needed to be paid, but as I turned to go back indoors I glanced at it almost with disinterest. The words thereon are indelibly printed on my brain ever since. **"Daddy died. Ten thirty this morning. Ring re arrangements".** The shock of learning that the big man was no longer going to be waiting for us to come on holiday, or ever again to listen to our tales, was too much to take in all at once. After five minutes I was ready to do the necessary. I took a bus to where my young sister Fran was working and asked to speak to her. It was really only when I told her and saw her reaction that the reality began to sink in. From there, we went to find Catch and the rest of the afternoon disappeared in a haze of telephone calls to home and travel agents and heaven knows where.

Late that night, we sat in Euston station waiting for

the Holyhead train to depart. Sitting in a bar, we didn't feel like drinking; just talking and trying to get used to the idea. Each one of us was almost afraid to leave the group, as if being alone was somehow wrong.

We had a very sad reunion at Dun Laoghaire the following morning and from there we travelled home to a sea of grief. The next two days were about the longest of my life. Sympathisers were coming and shaking hands and it seemed to me as if every one of them had a story to tell. Many of the stories I had heard already, while still more new ones were cropping up all the time On the day after the funeral I awoke to find the house still thronging with great neighbours and friends, all wanting to do whatever was needed. Throughout the morning I drank enough tea to re-float the Titanic and had enough ham sandwiches to sink it all the way to the bottom again. In the end I decided I needed to be alone. I borrowed the keys to "his car" and just drove off.

I turned left in the village where he had retired and drove along the Edenderry road to the gate that led to what was once our hill field. There I parked, and for the first time since arriving home, I heard the sound of silence. It was mid-June and, as I leaned on the gate looking at the barley which was just starting to turn, a whole lifetime of memories came back at once. Away in front of me was the low field where so often we had found a newly calved cow at the farthest point from the house. To my right was the bridge which led to the slang and the long field. I had been with him as a very small boy the day that he had made that bridge. I can still remember the fear I felt when the ass had inadvertently backed the cart with the two barrels into the drain, trapping him underneath. I was in a state of blind panic for I knew instinctively that there was nothing much I could do. Then, with a show of strength borne from desperation, he lifted the cart from his chest and managed to crawl from underneath. A lesser man might have been crushed. I saw himself then, on a crisp February evening, as he tilled this same field with the old Styer tractor, sitting spreadlegged at the wheel, drinking tea from the lemonade bottle which I had been sent with after school, a sandwich in one hand, his hat turned

Daddy, that big man who filled us with a great love of nature.

upside down on the ground at his side. I smiled as I remembered the ritualistic way he always ate bare-headed even when out doors on a cold day. I saw him throw back his head and laugh heartily at some story or other, which I had told him, and suddenly I realised that I was crying. Then, from the middle of that corn-field there came the throaty crow of a cock pheasant, proclaiming to the world that his brood was growing happily and that all would be ready for November the first. It seemed more fitting, just then, than a twenty-one gun salute.

CHAPTER TWELVE

Throughout my time in London, although there were no real opportunities to engage in the sport of shooting in any real sense, the love of the game never left me. The most homesick times, which I can remember, were invariably the first of November each year. Just to walk through the parks at that time and see the trees taking on their winter colours was enough to get the pulse racing and dream about what was happening at home. As the years passed, my focus changed. As I have already said I now had a wife, Breda, who had already decided that she had done enough travelling before she met me and, pretty soon she decided, so had I. The dreams of going on safari through darkest Africa and the Australian bush were not as important now. But along the way I had picked up other dreams, which would lead me in directions not yet travelled by our family. There was a television series which I used to watch about country life and hobbies. I am not sure who the man was who gave the demonstrations, but each week he dealt with a different topic; from fishing and shooting to making jam and varnishing blackthorn walking sticks. He covered more topics than I could ever hope to remember, but two shows in particular remained with me.

The first of those was about how to train a gundog, and that evening he won my heart. To see that lovely black Labrador walking to heel, and only running to retrieve when told, then returning and sitting waiting for the bird to be accepted, was something else. Never before had I imagined that this was possible. The level of understanding between man and dog was awesome. The apparent simplicity of the training method which he used, however, understated the time and dedication required. Right then and there I resolved that, one day, I would train a dog to that standard. Little though I knew about the task, I did realize that it was something which Daddy would have admired, but would never have contemplated trying.

The second TV show, which really caught my fancy, was dedicated to catching wild brown trout on an artificial fly. Bear in mind that this was something which we, in the Midlands, had never seen done, although Daddy had known enough about it to believe that you had to be born with a fly rod in your hand to ever master it. As I watched, he explained the rudiments of the art. He started by showing the rod and line and then started flicking the line to and fro, with all the ease of a magician. Then he waded into a fast flowing stream about eighteen inches deep and the camera picked up the rise of a fish. He explained a few things about how to position himself downstream of the fish, and cast the fly to a point just upstream and let it float down. Then the camera picked up the trout, lying just below the surface. He looked like a little lightweight boxer as he darted just a few inches in either direction searching for food, occasionally taking something off the surface. Suddenly he took the artificial and the reel was screaming as he took off around the pool. He was a beautiful fish, of just over a pound weight, and long before the fight was over I was hooked forever.

This simply had to be the most graceful and delicate method of catching trout ever devised by man. I spent the rest of my time in London trying to find out as much as I could because I knew that as soon as I returned home, I would not rest until I could master this rare art. Access to trout fishing in London was restricted to reservoirs unless you had serious money so any attempt would have to wait until I came home. When we eventually decided to make the move to Ireland, it was 1982 and, before I left, I decided that I should buy a fly rod, reel and line for I was not at all sure that such advanced technology was yet available here. For good measure, I purchased a pair of waders and two books. One was about how to cast a fly and the other was all I would ever need to know about training a dog to work in the field. Little did I know as I brought my purchases back to my tiny flat, with its FOR SALE sign at the ready, that I was about to embark on two of the most frustrating and demanding tasks imaginable.

It was late July 1982 when we finally arrived on the "ould sod" and within about two months I took myself down to a local gun shop. The owner, when I had told him what I wanted and how much money I was prepared to spend, disappeared into a back room and came back with a shotgun in each hand. The first was an old English make with a very long stock which did not take my fancy at all. The other was a Baikal side by side and I liked it right away. I took it from him and mounted it to my shoulder, broke it open and squinted down the barrels, then checked for all-round tightness and decided then and there that this was the gun for me. After a bit of haggling he threw in a cartridge belt and cleaning kit. I was then introduced, through a friend, to the local gun club. This was a novel concept to me - before I had left home there was no such thing as a gun club, at least not in our area and now that I was living in the unfamiliar territory of Co. Kilkenny, it was a major boon to have a virtual free run of all the land in the parish. At least, those farms where the owner had given the go ahead. There were, of course, a few who refused permission and these in a peculiar way added some of the spice to my shooting over the following years.

As I had not yet found a permanant home for my family, it seemed unwise to consider buying a dog so, for that season, I was unable to do any serious shooting except for a couple of days with friends. The thing which I remember most about that year was, that on the few days when I did get out, I never actually shot anything. My only reply when challenged about this was that it would be different next year when I would have my own highly trained canine.

If you're fancy free it's the place to be.

CHAPTER THIRTEEN

It was in June of 1983 that I finally went on the hunt for a pup. After thinking about all the options, and the sort of shooting which I intended doing, I decided to go for either a Setter or an English Pointer. There were a few false starts when I took dogs out for trials and each time I was put off by something, usually either the price, or doubtful parentage, or a combination of both. Finally, I fell in love with a six-month-old pointer bitch and handed over the princely sum of forty pounds. Only then did I decide to start reading the book on how to train her. That was my first mistake, and I admit I made many. The real concept of dog training and forming a relationship with a dog had not entered my head at this stage. The book stated that the dog should be ready to start learning his trade at between six and nine months, but it should be remembered that this was in the context of a dog that had been with his owner from about ten or twelve weeks. This was all-important, as the dog would have learned to trust the owner to a degree. All I could see was the first of November looming and come hell or high water, we were going to shoot pheasants on the day.

Everything was rushed. After two or three days teaching her to respond to her name "Judy", I decided to take her out into a field close to where I was living and then I started to understand frustration. Trying to make her walk to heel on a lead was bad enough, but making her sit was next to impossible. Then I tried to walk away and leave her sitting, but of course she followed immediately and like the good book said, I shook her by the slack under her chin whereupon she promptly ran to her kennel. After several false starts I decided that this was a lesson which would be of little practical value in the field so I decided to skip it. Taking her for a run was great. She seemed to have all the right instincts in the way of hunting. The trouble started when I tried to call her off a scent. She would pay no attention whatever. This would make me mad so, whenever I did get her back, she got a telling off which, of course, did little to help this great new relationship along. The good book said that it was always necessary to walk any game off the training ground before starting the lesson. The reason for this was to avoid distracting her with juicy smells and let her concentrate on me. But nobody said anything about larks. Whenever they did flush they simply flew back over my head and landed behind me. Once Judy got a smell of them there was no chance that she was going to pay any attention to me until she had chased every last one of them to hell and back.

After about a fortnight of this I decided that the best thing was to ignore the advice of the book and go hunting. She enjoyed herself immensely and to be honest so did I. For the first time we were able to get along without me falling out with her. She hunted and quartered quite well, and picked up trail after trail without actually finding anything. I guessed that this would improve with time, and then suddenly she set in a field of rushes and every ounce of willpower I had was hoping for a cock. After about ten seconds, a hare bolted and all the whistling and shouting in the world would not bring her back. For the next fifteen minutes, I had to stand idly by and be content with the occasional glimpse as she passed some distant gap at full speed without ever seeing the hare. Eventually she came back with a very happy look about her and I did not have the heart to scold her.

Sometimes, when she was quartering, I found that if I walked in a different direction and gave a toot on the whistle, she would look in my direction and actually take a hand signal. This represented something of a breakthrough for me and my confidence began to rise. I also learned that, when I made a fuss of her on her return, it got better results than constant scolding. Still, there were many times when I just sat down in the field and felt salty tears run down my cheeks as she raced in whatever direction took her fancy. Then one day in late September, it finally happened. We were hunting a field of freshly cut barley stubble and, as usual, the larks were driving me to my wits end when suddenly she set in a way that was different to anything she had done before. There was a definite purpose to her stance; rigid from nose to tail with a peculiar furrow in her brow which I had not noticed before. Although I was to see that furrow many times over the next seven or eight years, each time it signified the same thing - pheasants.

This time, however, I did as the book had suggested and talked to her soothingly, for even I knew instinctively that this was it. As the seconds dragged by, I was eagerly scanning the stubbles for sight of the bird. All at once the clutch erupted, eight or nine in all. Not yet furnished enough to tell if they were cocks or hens. Weak in flight, they were barely able to cross the first ditch and get out of sight as Judy ran riot in every direction, lest there were any more of these strange and exciting creatures to be found. When she finally came back, my tears were of pure joy as we rolled on the ground and I tickled her belly and told her what a fantastic, clever, intelligent mutt she really was. The feeling of elation which I got stayed with me for a long while after. Now I knew that I was on the right track. This animal was going to make the difference between coming home with a bag full of game and a bag full of nothing.

As the weeks dragged on, I spent every spare moment I had in the field, still trying to put manners on her and falling out regularly, but every time she went away on her own and flushed a cock I felt it was down to my handling. As opening day approached, I lost all sense of real life and concentrated on every aspect of preparation. The gun was cleaned repeatedly, the belt filled with shells, only to be rechecked to see that they were all the right number. Boots and bag were kept just inside the back door. I spent most of the night twisting and turning, finally falling into an uneasy sleep shortly before dawn. The clock jarred me into consciousness at six-thirty. I was up and moving in minutes.

After a hasty breakfast, I stepped out into the crisp November dawn and after a short drive released the excited bitch to take on the pheasant world. She hunted fine for the first half hour without any sort of find and then resorted to running around my legs and rolling over on her back, looking to play. This was not what I had been looking forward to and suddenly we were fighting again. She seemed to sulk for a bit and then went about her business. She picked up a trail at the edge of a field of stubbles, and worked it for several minutes without success. She vanished into heavy cover and for several minutes I was listening as she worked her way through, expecting at any moment to hear the excited crowing of a cock coming my way. Nothing. I worked along a couple of likely looking ditches and finally she set solid.

The furrow was there on her brow and I knew we were in luck. She was in a drain and there was just no escape for this one. As soon as I was ready I urged her forward, only to flush a hen. My heart sank but suddenly I remembered that the law of averages meant that I was more likely to get red feathers next time. We hunted diligently until twelve o'clock and she flushed two more hens, rather haphazardly and I decided to give it best and break for lunch. The sympathetic reception I received at home did little to cheer me. I was totally determined to succeed before nightfall.

After lunch I went to fresh ground and was a bit pleased that, although I had been hearing firing in all directions, I had not yet met any other shooters. As I stepped into a field of beet I got lucky and spotted two cocks picking on the headland, some seventy yards away. They spotted me at the same time and slouched quietly into the hedge. Judy was already hunting the beet for all she was worth and all the whistling and excited waving in the world couldn't get her to the spot. I ran to where the birds were and hoped to flush one of them myself but to no avail. Finally, she came along the headland and passed by without getting a smell. Twenty yards along the ditch she went, and back again, then went back to hunting the beet without a care in the world. Tears welled up in my eyes and the thought of putting her down then and there was tempting to say the least. Suddenly a lovely young cock flushed at her nose while she was still running flat out and she took off after him, and was gone for twenty minutes. When she returned, she got a very severe telling off. By now my legs were getting heavy and the rest of the afternoon slipped by with thoughts of what sort of dog I would buy next.

At about four-thirty she picked up a trail at the edge of some rushes and after working the scent for a few minutes, she set dead at the corner of the field. I stood some ten yards off her and urged her to flush. She refused to budge. As the minutes ticked by, I moved closer and stood with my legs either side of her, gently pushing her forward. Then out he came.

Struggling to clear the undergrowth, falling over himself and flying straight past me, forcing me to turn through one hundred and eighty degrees to cover him. He was a beautifully furnished young cock flying straight away from me; my favourite type of shot at that time. I gave him what I thought was the proper distance, and missed with both barrels, or, as they say in the Midlands, "I never gave him a dust". I just stood there and stared as the bird flew the full length of the field and crossed the road into the wood, there to roost for the night. When I looked back I saw Judy watching me reproachfully. I could see that she thought it was my turn for a good shake. As I reached the car, the dusk was gathering and the sudden sound of a cock crowing as he went to roost, somehow seemed to lift my spirits as I realized that I had a whole lifetime ahead of me and that things could only get better.

On the following Saturday I was out with the dawn, with Judy looking very business-like as she galloped up and down the lane-way, sniffing the ditches on either side until we came to a gate and crossed into a field of beet. As my feet touched the ground, she set. Rigid. In an instant, a young cock was struggling to get airborne and as I lifted the gun to my shoulder I got tangled in the bag. Blind panic threatened to take over completely, and as I righted myself for a shot, he was fast approaching the forty-yard mark. I fired more in hope than expectation and suddenly he was down. Only winged, he was running and the thought of losing him was enough to bring me to my knees in an attempt to spot him. Judy, however, with all the self-assurance of an old hand was on the trail in a flash and suddenly I saw her head go down as she caught him just short of the headland. She just held him there until I took him from her. My day was made.

From that moment, she could do as she pleased for the next few hours. I was just too happy knowing that I would be able to show off a bird. She flushed another cock, which I did not get a shot at, and several hens, before lunch. Midway through the afternoon she did some really wonderful work in a field of rushes, and when the cock finally broke I was ready for him. I killed him clean with the first shot and as I picked him up I knew that this was not a young bird. This was a trophy winner. When I measured him at home later, he was thirty-seven inches from beak to tail and to this day, remains the cock by which all others are measured. As that season progressed, Judy was growing in confidence and, more and more, we were able to shoot as a team without falling out although she had already developed the habit of hunting her way and expecting me to follow. Hardly surprising, given the kind of training she had had.

Of course the dark evenings gave me a great opportunity to study the book in great detail and, the more I read, the more I realized where I had gone wrong.

Losing patience with a pup is a definite no-no, and once you go down that road there is no way back. She had become somewhat afraid that she might do the wrong thing and once she felt that she was due a telling off, she would just stay away until she knew I had cooled off. I managed to get her to walk on the lead reasonably well and, to sit when told, but to go away and leave her was not on. I did not realize the importance of this until later, when I got into the habit of shooting duck ponds, during the course of my ramblings. The ability to leave her sitting while I crept forward would have been infinitely preferable to approaching with herself straining at the lead, as she invariably was.

The more I read that book, the more I began to realize the fundamental importance of building a relationship with the animal, based on complete trust. Thus I soon learned the folly of trying to rush her training schedule. The principle of the book was, simply, to repeat each exercise, time and again, and insist that the dog obey until the penny would finally drop. There was simply no point in moving on to the next exercise until she had completely mastered the last. Teaching her to remain sitting while I moved farther and farther away and stayed away longer each time and eventually moved out of sight was really about building confidence in her to know that I would always return. What I lacked in experience, she made up for in cuteness as the years went on. Her nose was as good as any I have ever seen since and her work rate was never in question. During that first season I would say that we hunted pretty much every field in our club area, and quite a few besides, and by Christmas we had bagged thirteen cocks, which I was more than pleased with.

Many birds did escape, however, because hunting then as now was a two man sport. Pheasants are wily birds, all the more so as the season progresses and they know instinctively how to make use of any bit of cover to escape. When a bird is lying in the relative security of a ditch, a lone shooter has little chance. Birds will rarely flush on your side so you end up trying to cover both sides at once. With two partners, it becomes a simple matter to decide who goes where and, on balance, everyone gets a shot from time to time. As that season progressed, I was getting to know, more and more, a man who was married to my wife's first cousin. His name was Tommy Walton. We had known each other a relatively short time and he was at the same stage with shooting as I was. That is to say, this was his first season and he was in the process of training a young dog, a lovely English Springer bitch ironically also named Judy. He was in a different club to me and he, too, was looking for a partner.

It was not until St. Stephen's day that we finally managed to get together. It was a beautiful, crisp morning and we opted to go to an area which was actually outside the reach of either of our clubs, but where he felt he had some dubious permission to shoot. It turned out to be some of the best pheasant country I ever saw and, in the years that followed, we had consistent shooting there all through every season. But on that morning we could not foresee any of this. We were simply out for a day's hunting and each eager to impress. On the first ditch, which we hunted, the springer became excited and Tommy called to me to "watch up". Suddenly a woodcock appeared over the top of the trees, flying back over my head and diving towards the ground at an almighty speed. I was more than pleased to see him fall at the first shot. Five minutes later, as we approached the end of that field, Tommy shot a cock at long range and when I saw the springer moments later, struggling back across the ploughed ground, with the bird in her mouth, I fell in love with the little bitch.

As we walked we talked, and it was obvious that we both liked shooting for the same sort of reasons. We were both young and fit and, the long hard walking and muscle testing exercise of jumping drains and racing to a set dog, were more important to either of us than the actual shooting. We also found that the conversation flowed freely and before long we were making plans to try our hand at grouse shooting the following September. When my Judy set in the farthest corner of a stubble field, some eighty yards distant, we sprinted flat out, without the need for either of us to make a decision. I approached the dog while Tommy made for a gap in the ditch where he could just about squeeze through. As he reached the other side, a cock flushed and once again was shot first time. Almost immediately another came out my side and met with a similar fate. The omens were really looking good. As we tucked the birds safely in the bags, we smiled and agreed to form a partnership. It was sealed with a firm handshake, but neither of us could have imagined then that it would turn out to be one of the sweetest and most rewarding friendships we would ever have.

CHAPTER FOURTEEN

O 'tis a wondrous web we weave
When first we practise to deceive the wary trout.
But if we're made of proper stuff
And practise long and hard enough, 'twill straighten
out.

I have no idea who penned that verse. I do, however, know without doubt that long before he ever straightened the line he pulled a lot of hair from his head prematurely. How else would he write such beautiful poetry if he had not endured the trials and tribulations of this most exciting, fascinating and yet exasperating of all sports. Sometime in the late spring or early summer of 1984 I decided the time was ripe for me to take the river by storm. I had already enjoyed a few pleasant mornings with my new partner, Tommy, fishing with worms when there was a fresh in the river. To be honest we had a fair measure of success. So with those few brownie points in the bag, I felt that I could afford to return empty-handed, on a few occasions, without being noticed.

I took the fly-rod from the press, fitted the reel and wondered. All the articles which I had read had told me all about which fly line I should start with, and what way to secure it to the reel and all about leaders and what-have-you. Suddenly, my mind was a total blank and the thought of going into a local tackle shop unnerved me completely. Luckily I was in the habit of travelling the country at the time so I opted for a quiet little shop, far from home, where no one would ever see me again. It was a Tuesday afternoon when I entered the shop and fortunately it was empty except for the proprietor. A man, probably in his sixties, with a ready smile was only too willing to help once I had explained the situation. He first fitted a backing line to the reel and explained the purpose of this. The drum of the reel was quite small and if the fly line were attached directly to it, it would take an awful lot of winds of the handle to retrieve line. "Forget" said he "the notion of a trout running downstream and stripping your fly line off. In the rivers hereabouts that will rarely be a problem".

Suddenly I found myself liking this man and we spent the next two hours happily, as teacher and student, while he patiently demonstrated the proper method of making up tapered leaders for the dry fly and leaders with droppers for wet fly fishing. I wanted to buy a knotless tapered leader, like the magazines had so often recommended for easy assembly, but he assured me this way was best. Spend a few bob now, he counselled, and the few spools of line will stand you in good stead for a long time to come. The thing which amazed me was that, for all the joinings of line which he recommended, there was only one knot-the full blood. There was one other very simple knot for attaching the fly to the leader. There was just no end to his patience as he watched over my ridiculous attempts to make all the different fingers push all the ends of the line through all the special hoops, which I was supposed to create. By the time I left the shop I did at least have a clear idea in my head of what was required. Only practise was required for perfection. I bought a few other odds and ends, including a landing net, and what seemed to me to be enough flies to last for that season at least. Late that night, when the family was in bed and the house was quiet I started to practise those knots in earnest. Sitting at the table with just one spool of line and a nail clippers, I tied one knot after another, time and again until at last the idea was fixed in my head so I decided it was safe to go to bed. For several more nights I practised until I had the technique off to a fine art. Well, almost. I knew that if I was to have any success at the bank side it would be necessary to have the fundamentals sorted out first.

The next step was to find a secluded stretch of river where I could thrash the water to my heart's content, without having the entire population of Kilkenny looking at me. For that reason, I travelled out through the village of Kells to the Kings River on what was a beautiful early summer evening. The sky was clear and blue with the sun still high when I arrived at about six thirty and all along the river I could see trout splashing and rising and, of course, knew nothing of the fact that they were at best only sprats. The evening rise was something which I had no real concept of at that time. I pulled on the waders and the fishing vest and cap and set up the rod. Then, with my shiny new landing net neatly clipped to my belt, I waded straight into the water and began casting upstream. Or rather trying to.

The rod was waving about like a demented windmill and occasionally I would hear the line cracking like a whip which I assumed was what I was supposed to be doing. The only snag was that it was not happening very often. I could get the line up in the air all right, but found it hard to remember when to let it fall on the water. Sometimes it fell of it's own accord, either in front of me or behind me or sometimes on the bank. There were a few times when it snagged the back of my fishing vest and then there was the problem of trying to disentangle it, without losing my balance in a fast flowing current which was threatening to throw me headlong downstream. Of course it never occurred to me to try fishing from the bank.! I think I felt that was for amateurs. Eventually I got a kind of rhythm going, whereby I could flash the line to and fro in the air for a time and then throw it out in front. Although it was landing in something of a heap and no matter how far I waded upstream, the trout seemed to always rise out of range. For all my lack of success at catching fish, I was thoroughly enjoying myself and consoled myself with the thought that once I mastered the cast, the catching of those innocent trout would be childsplay.

My arms grew tired, my shoulders and neck ached and eventually I decided to rest. I clambered onto the bank and sat down to let the birds do the work for a while. Listening to the birdsong and watching the fish splashing all along the water while the sun was setting at my back was, and I suppose still is, the most enchanting form of relaxation I know. I tried a few more casts for luck and when I finally drove home I was singing with sheer pleasure. Of course I had no fish, but that was because they were simply not biting.

After several more excursions with much the same results, I got lucky in that it was recommended that I try a video, which could be hired from a local rental store. They were the great new rage at that time. This guy gave a very clear demonstration of the technique and explained about all the principles which were involved in casting a fly. Watching it all in slow motion was a real revelation, and after several hours of playing and rewinding, I began to get a pretty decent idea about what I was actually trying to do. Back to the water I went, and after an hour's practise I found that I had improved so much that my arms no longer ached and the casting was becoming something of a pleasure. I was casting a longer line and even attempting to shoot that extra loop and when I faced downstream the pull of the current was enough to compensate for any slackness in my performance. I still knew nothing about the difference between wet and dry fly fishing and had no idea at all about what fly I should be using.

The nearest I had to a system of fly selection was to go into a tackle shop and study the fly display boxes. Whichever pattern seemed to be in short supply I deemed to be what everyone else was using. The fact that occasionally a suicidal sprat managed to impale himself on the hook gave me the encouragement to go on. I began to fish later into the dusk and found that the fish were more inclined to feed seriously, thrashing the surface of the water with ferocity, which made me believe that there was just no way one could repeatedly throw a fly with a hook in it without catching regularly. That was when the true meaning of the word "frustrated" began to emerge. The times I stood there with fish rising all around me and covering first one, then another, and losing the rhythm, snagging the fly on a branch of a tree and sometimes going over the depth of the waders in my haste to retrieve it. All around me I could hear that demoralizing slurping sound as the trout fed on merrily. When I finally caught a fish, as distinct from a sprat, on the fly I was sorely tempted to have it mounted, never mind the fact that he was just over half a pound. I began to ask questions of the many anglers I met and I should say that, without exception, they were open enough to tell me what they were using. Of course, as often as not, they were not catching anything to get excited about either, but at least now I felt like I was actually fishing.

Then, quite by chance, I met one Johnny Meany. Fly-tier extraordinaire. We got talking and as soon as I discovered that he knew anything at all about this game, I asked as casually as I knew how, about the problem of selecting a suitable fly. "There is no easy way" he told me, "except to learn". He invited me to join his fly-tying class and when I looked doubtfully at my rather stubby fingers, he assured me that they were no handicap at all. That course, as well as being a whole lot of fun, turned out to be one of the best things I ever undertook. I found myself back in a classroom with about fifteen others who all appeared to lack any degree of dexterity whatever at first. But by and large we all managed to put fur and feather and heaven knows what else onto a hook in a couple of sessions. But along the way, Johnny taught us so much more, starting with the difference between wet and dry fishing he explained the process of catching a trout in three simple steps. 1. Approach, 2. Presentation and 3. Fly selection. After you have managed all that, he said, hooking and landing the fish is simply the coup de grace.

1. The Approach

Once a trout has been seen to rise, the first problem is always to decide from where to cast to him. This will be dictated by several factors including current, bank-side vegetation and even the depth at which the fish is lying. The closer a fish is to the surface the closer it will be possible to come to him. However, there is no point in arriving at the chosen spot only to find that the little darling has left a bow-wave pointing upstream. Learning to stalk a fish is a study all of its own. The eyes of a trout are set so that he can use binocular vision "two eyed" to observe a narrow field of vision directly in front. This he uses to great effect to hunt and observe what food the current will bring his way. He can see for anything up to fifteen to twenty feet and judge distance with great accuracy. However, each eye can also be used separately to view what is happening on either side. This is called monocular vision. In this mode, the trout can see movement quite clearly, but has no real judgement of distance. What this means in practice is that when an angler is standing in line with a fish he can move cautiously closer without alarming it. To the trout's eye, the object will not appear closer. Any movement in an up or down-stream direction will set the alarm bells ringing. For this reason the waving of arms and suchlike should be avoided like the plague.

The trout's window is a phenomenon not widely understood. This is the small patch of water directly over his head, through which he looks at our world. Imagine, if you will, that the trout lives in a world which looks like an inverted cone, with the top section cut off. The part of the cone, which is all around him, is the extent of his vision underwater and is like a mirror in that it shows him a perfect reflection of the bed of the river. The hole in the top of the cone, directly above his head, is his window, the size of which will vary depending on the depth at which he is lying. The angle of his vision as he looks up is ninety-seven degrees and so, the deeper he sinks down, the wider will be the window. It is also necessary to understand the effect of refraction on light rays, because, as the trout looks through that window, his line of vision is effectively bent so that he can now see at a much wider angle into our world. This is best demonstrated by putting a coin in a basin and then standing back to a point from where the coin is not visible. Then, have someone fill the basin with water and the coin will rise up as if by magic. Unfortunately, the same magic works for the trout and this is why it is sometimes necessary to fish from a kneeling position.

Anything which is below thirty degrees from the outer edge of his window, is really just a blur to the fish. It is interesting to note that a fish has a complete blind spot directly behind him. This corresponds exactly to his binocular vision up front. Fish do not hear sounds as we do, but they are very sensitive to vibrations such as a heavy footstep or something scraping on the bottom of a boat. This explains why the old hunting adage "walk little, look much" is so important. Stalking trout is a fascinating pastime in its own right. Over the years I have spent many happy hours moving very slowly and getting as close as possible to watch their behaviour.

2. Presentation

Presentation, like stalking, is a skill which when learned becomes automatic. The gentle art of casting a fly, when executed properly, is a joy to behold. Watching it done badly is irksome in the extreme. Good casting tuition is freely available these days and should be availed of more often because, apart from putting more fish in the bag, it also makes the whole business more enjoyable. To be able to place the artificial fly approximately eighteen inches in front of the fish's nose, and let it float naturally without any drag, is all-important. Should the water drag the line, and thus the fly, then the exercise will be a waste of time, except on occasions when fishing sedges, when the fly may be dragged deliberately to create a wake, just like the real thing. Once these two parts of the process have been perfected then the matter of catching the fish becomes simply a matter of offering him the correct artificial.

3. Fly selection

This can be far from simple for the novice. After years of trying it is, for me, still a question of trial and error with the results always in doubt until some foolhardy trout offers to commit suicide. Then, of course, I convince myself that it was all due to good judgement. Johnny introduced us to emergence charts, which opened up the possibility of a completely new hobby – entomology. The starting point here has to be the breaking down of the flies into four different groups. These are the up-winged flies, flies with roof shaped wings, flat-winged flies and hard-winged flies. The first two of these are by far the most important to the fly fisher and incorporate the olives and sedges.

Johnny then showed us another trick, which I was amazed to find that I had not noticed in all my hours at the riverbank, namely the different ways in which trout rise, depending on what they are feeding on. The principle being that any animal in the wild will only expend as much energy on catching food as is absolutely necessary. Also, he will not expend more energy than he can hope to recoup by catching it. With this knowledge, it becomes possible to make an educated guess at whether he is feeding on duns or spinners. The latter, being dying and helpless, can be picked ever so gently from the surface, while the former are lively and likely to fly off at any moment thus causing a more energetic rise. Sedges too, when migrating towards the bank at dusk, leave a little wake behind them and this disturbance of the surface seems to drive the trout into a frenzy.

At one point I encountered a problem which threatened to break my resolve entirely. I was fishing a stretch of fast water where, late in the evening, the fish would turn the water into a churning mess for all of about forty-five minutes, just before dusk. The rise was so vicious that I expected to see sedges as big as blackbirds leaving the water in droves, but no matter how hard I looked I could see nothing in the air or on the water. Frantically, I moved up and down the river, casting first to one fish, then another and back again to the first as soon as he rose again, frequently getting myself tangled in a hopeless mess and almost crying with frustration and tying on every sedge in the box without an offer. For weeks this went on and I was beginning to think that "fishlessitis" was to be my lot forever more. Eventually I paid a visit to my old friend Johnny and laid the problem on the table before him.

He smiled that patient smile, which adults usually reserve for children, and told me to think. Repeatedly I banged the table with my clenched fists and threatened to pull my hair out then and there. Finally he told me that what I thought was the trout's head was actually his tail slashing at the surface while he was taking ascending nymphs some inches below the surface. Oh, the calm and tranquility that that simple revelation brought to my life is indescribable. Once I became aware of this much my curiosity was aroused and no amount of literature was enough to satisfy me from then on. Now when I get home from an evening's fishing, I invariably spoon the contents of a trout's stomach, place it in a dish of water and poke around at it checking it with a magnifying glass to try to understand more.

Few people can fail to be moved by the sight of a chick hatching from an egg. At least the few who have ever been lucky enough to have observed it happening. I frequently look at hundreds of little nymphs in the dish which have been taken by the trout in the very act of shedding their outer skins and it is like watching a frozen picture of a desperate struggle for survival. A struggle which these flies have lost but which millions will have survived. Likewise the trout on the sink, awaiting the pan, has also lost the battle but many more will live on to fight another day.

For anyone wishing to learn about these things there are any number of good books on the market, but I would recommend John Goddard's "Waterside Guide" which is a pocket-sized guide to all the insects which one finds at the river or lake. Also "The Trout and the Fly. A new approach" by Brian Clarke and John Goddard is a fabulous study of all aspects of the sport, especially stalking the fish. It should be noted that I make no claim whatever to any degree of expertise in these matters. I mention it only in the hope that I may stir someone's interest and that they too might have the same fun and frustration as me. I wish you luck.

CHAPTER FIFTEEN

In September 1984 Tommy and I made good the promise to shoot grouse on Sliabh na mBan. It was the day before the Centenary Hurling Final in Thurles. At that time, Tommy worked part time in a pub and on the Friday night before we launched our assault the slagging in the pub was serious. Older and wiser men who had spent many a fruitless day trudging the mountain, without ever firing a shot, were only too happy to laugh and tell us we were wasting our time. There were even those who suggested that we would require a good deal of luck to return at all and that there were so many dangers up there that there should be a law against amateurs like us going up.

We spent the early morning scouting around the base of the mountain trying to find a place to start climbing from. Finally we parked the old Renault Four and shook hands as we started going up through the trees. After about ten minutes the pain from our exertions was becoming unbearable and for a few minutes we considered giving up but the thought of the reception we would get back at the pub was what we needed to keep us climbing. When we finally broke out of the trees and saw the vast expanse of heather we felt a tremendous sense of achievement and waited for a long moment to enjoy the view. Then we just struck out in no particular direction wondering between ourselves what kind of heather the grouse were likely to be found on.

The old timers had given us so many tips that we reckoned we were better off ignoring them altogether. The two dogs were doing their business in what seemed to be a satisfactory manner with the pointer quartering at a fairly fast pace and the spaniel was working close at hand. Secretly we were both hoping that our own dog would be the first to find birds but after about an hour had passed without a smell we began to question our sanity. At times the walking was easy enough and then quite suddenly the terrain would change to being very rocky with many deep and dangerous crevices or alternately the heather would become so long that we were constantly sinking in the stuff. At other times we would find ourselves in soft young heather where at least the walking was pleasant. Suddenly my Judy set some distance in front of us and there was a scramble to get into position for a shot. The springer, also named Judy, then got in on the act and started working out the strange smell, which was assailing her nostrils.

The pointer was rigid as the springer pushed on some ten yards and suddenly they broke, a covey of six birds on our right and flying at such an angle that denied me any chance of a shot as Tommy was more or less in my line of fire. Tommy only had time to fire one quick shot before they disappeared over a ridge, but that one shot was all he needed. The bird tumbled and without waiting to be sent the springer made the retrieve. At first we were just too excited to admire the bird properly. The feeling of elation was unbelievable. No matter what happened for the rest of the day we could now go home with our heads up and never again listen to the nonsense which had been hurled at us the previous night.

The fact that Tommy had shot the bird did nothing to dampen my feelings. That was a trait which was always evident in our shooting and over the following years was part of why we became such great friends. We literally hugged each other there on the mountain.

It was several minutes before we were able to continue and when we finally got ourselves together we headed in the direction that the remaining birds had taken. We only travelled a mere few hundred yards when the dogs picked up the scent again and this time there were only five birds in the covey. When they flushed this time they were straight in front of us and we both got a shot. The bird which I picked decided to turn to fly with the wind just as I was about to fire and suddenly I found him escaping at an alarming speed. He fell among rocks and so busy was I keeping my eye on the spot where he fell that I ignored the chance of a left and right. In all the years that we have hunted grouse subsequently, I have never had another opportunity to shoot a left and right.

At that same moment Tommy had shot his second bird and this time our excitement was unbounded because he was so happy to see me get a grouse. We walked with a spring in our step for the remainder of the day and the fact that we saw no further sign of the quarry was of no consequence whatever. By the time we got back to the car we were well and truly jaded and only too glad to change out of our wellies and remove the gunbelts. As we wended our way back towards civilization, we found an old country pub and decided that a couple of pints of shandy were in order. There were four or five locals already inside, playing rings, who greeted us warmly on entry. When they heard where we had come from they were all interested to hear about how we had fared out and for a while the craic was mighty. At one stage Tommy suggested to me rather quietly that we might make some handy money if we were to challenge them to a few games.

The standard was, to say the least, poor. But I

declined saying that they were making me tired just looking at them picking the rings off the floor. In the time that we were there I don't think they managed to hang more than a half dozen rings in all. The first couple of pints went down without ever touching the sides and when we finally left for home, we felt like Moses returning from the Mountain in triumph. On the following day I believe I became a member of a pretty exclusive club when I went to the Centenary Hurling Final in Thurles, with grouse sandwiches for lunch. Sadly my luck did not hold and the result of the game is history, which I, as an avid Offaly supporter, would prefer to forget. In the weeks that followed, we went for a few sorties looking for duck, but our eye was firmly on the first of November. We were determined to prove that we had the dogs and the ability to shoot as good as anybody.

Another reason why Tommy and I enjoyed shooting together was the issue of safety. When shooting with a partner, it is of vital importance that both parties are responsible and safe. Things tend to happen quite suddenly in the field and anyone who is prone to rash movements will not last long. Or, at least their partner won't. In our case we both had the utmost respect for guns and at all times were aware of danger. This becomes vital when two individuals are on opposite sides of cover and usually out of sight of each other. It will also be necessary to run and jump drains in a hurry and such situations leave no room for error. Through the years we developed such an understanding about how to cover a set dog so as to cut off all escape routes for a bird, without ever compromising safety, and I suppose it was just part of the special bond between us.

Catch, my brother, had returned from London at the same time as myself and was living and working in Dublin. From that year on, he came to Kilkenny for the first of the pheasant shooting and occasionally one or two other days during the season. From 1985 on, he was also a regular on the trip to the mountain. It was, of course, unthinkable that we would shoot on the first day without finishing the day with a social evening and some of those evenings will remain in the memory for far longer than any birds which were bagged on the day. The fun in the pub was largely due to the fact that all other shooting men were out on the same day and the old bit of competition is the spice of good sport. This, mixed with the fact that some of the regulars, who although they were only too willing to accept a bird for the table, would happily try to wind us up about the morals of shooting at poor defenseless birds which could not shoot back.

The arguments and debates which we had in the pub were priceless. All the more so as the night wore on. It was during one such debate that I received inspiration to try my hand at writing. I was taking no active part in the discussion but rather listening to how the arguments were going to and fro. I felt that no amount of point-scoring was going to convince anybody, who was anything like a conscientious objector, so I began to think about the possibility of writing a poem. That was on the night of the grouse shooting, i.e. the first of September and on the first of November in a similar state of inebriation, I recited the poem which has since been published called "Ode to the Anti's". It was so well received that someone suggested that I should write a book. Of course at that time of the night all things seem eminently possible and I assured all and sundry that I would do so. For one reason or another, many a year was to pass before I would eventually put pen to paper.

Also in those early years there was a former shooting partner of Tommy's who used to come with us particularly on the first of the season. His name was Paddy Dunne and he has since become moderately famous as the proprietor of a fishing tackle shop called "Hook, Line and Sinker". As a fourth man, he enabled us to form into two pairs and that in it's own way gave rise to no end of competition. For four consecutive years we used to buy a trophy between the four of us and have a competition for the longest bird on the first day. This in turn gave rise to some great fun as we argued in the pub about who had the longest tail and the rights and wrongs of how it was acquired. In the four years that we ran that, we each won one trophy as luck would have it, but in the end we decided to give it a miss as it was making some of us a little unsporting, to say the least. Nonetheless, it provided some great moments and, in my case at least, the only trophy of my adult life and one which I value highly.

As the years went on Tommy and myself became great friends and a great shooting partnership developed. The hours spent walking were an ideal chance to talk about all the problems of life while simply watching the two dogs working. The dogs seemed to enjoy each others company also and worked together without any sign of jealousy. Along the way we got to know quite a lot of the farmers over whose lands we were shooting. Many of these were great individuals, a few were less than welcoming and we were never great ones for respecting boundaries. Our motto was simply to start from a base where we knew we were welcome and just travel around at will. On the occasions that we were challenged, I was usually the one to do the talking and on more than one occasion this resulted in us gaining acceptance.

Tommy used to marvel at the way that I would simply break the gun when we were approached and start to apologize profusely, saying that we had not known that we had strayed too far. Then I would attempt to strike up a conversation about whatever came to mind, usually the prime state of his livestock or the lovely way that he kept his farm in trim and we would often stand chatting for up to half an hour. Occasionally it failed, but even then the most he would do would be to ask us to leave. There was, however, one aspect of country life which was more and more impinging on our sport. That was the effect of the land reclamation which was going on at that time. It seemed at times that almost every Sunday we would see the machinery that was doing away with still more cover, as whole farms were in some cases bulldozed into single fields. This at a time when, in Europe as a whole, we were creating mountains of beef and butter and God knows what else, while farmers were being encouraged through grants to leave land lying fallow. It always seemed like a terrible policy to be getting rid of so much good game habitat and although it was not the farmers who were to blame we did, in some ways, feel resentful.

For my part, I was more and more inclined to question the right of farmers to own shooting rights to land, since the birds were free to fly to any field they wished. I also felt, and still do, that as a shooting man I hold a licence to shoot game, which is issued by the State. I question the right of anybody to simply preserve game without showing me in writing, where he gets the authority from. This issue came to a head in one case, although it was fishing rights which were at stake. I was leaving the river one evening when I was approached by a farmer who asked me very gruffly if I had been fishing. Given that I was wearing waders and carrying a rod and landing net, the question seemed superfluous. He then went on to tell me that there was no fishing permitted there.

The sheer arrogance of his manner caused me to respond in a manner which I would not normally adopt. I asked him to show me, in writing, evidence that he owned the fishing rights. He was a new owner, and locals had fished the section of river since time began. Over the course of the next two years he had several angry confrontations with not only myself, but also several other anglers. He always refused to show that he owned the fishing rights. It so happened that, in the course of my work I was spending a lot of time in Dublin and I decided to do some investigating. The local County Council were able to confirm to me that the land was not rated as a fishery, but this was not enough to prove that he did not own the fishing rights. So I next went to the Land Registry Office in Dublin and there I found the Ordnance Survey Section where I could look at maps of the area in question. Having identified the land, I could then pay something like thirty pence to access the file. That was when things became interesting. I discovered that all the surrounding land had at one time been part of an old estate which was sold in separate lots sometime in the 1800's and at that time there was an indenture signed, stating that the hunting, hawking and fishing rights remained with the vendor. This information led me to the belief that many farmers were claiming gaming rights, which they actually do not own.

In that particular case, the gentleman involved simply gave in to the constant stream of anglers, myself included, who just persevered and fished to our hearts' content. As the years passed, I became more and more of the opinion that the concept of gaming rights was flawed. The idea that any individual or group can own such rights, to the exclusion of all others, seems contrary to democracy in my mind. I should however make it clear here that I never could countenance the argument that a farmer on whose land we happened to be should owe us any duty of care. I firmly believe, and always did, that if any recreational land-user wants to be insured against any accident, then it is up to the individual to organize insurance for him or her self. I also believe that the confusion, which abounds in this area, was contributed to, in no small way, by the legal profession. From their perspective, in any law case the solicitor acting for both sides will be paid in any event, regardless of who pays. It also strikes me that the word acting is very appropriate in this sense.

CHAPTER SIXTEEN

Although we did encounter a fair amount of hassle during our time, it is worth saying that by far the greater number of farmers were "salt of the earth" types. Most of them recognized us for what we were; people with a genuine love of the land and all the animals on it. On many occasions, we came across livestock in distress. Whether it was simply a ewe caught in bushes or lying on her back, which could be fatal if not sorted, we would always put things right before moving on. More serious problems, such as a beast stuck in a drain or whatever, we would always report.

I well remember one occasion when in midsummer I was just out for a ramble with the gun, hoping for a shot at a rabbit, when I found a bull in difficulty. He had a chain dangling from the ring in his nose and it had become entangled in a "ragworth" – a poisonous yellow weed. How long he had been there I have no idea, but by walking around in circles, he had succeeded in shortening the chain to about eighteen inches and was trapped with his head firmly anchored to the ground. Despite his immense strength he was totally unable to uproot the fragile weed, such is the effect of a ring on a bull. His eyes were bulging with terror and, although I have a very healthy respect for bulls, I could not bring myself to walk away. I was a long way from any kind of assistance. He was about thirty yards from the nearest ditch and there was a convenient gap which was fenced with barbed wire, three strands high. Cautiously, I studied the situation and decided to empty the gun and leave it outside the wire first. Then I crouched low and approached, keeping the ditch at my back, knowing that it was my only chance of escape if things got nasty. I spoke soothingly to him as I crawled, but my sweat glands were working overtime. I had planned to unwind the chain but thought better of it and simply pulled the "ragworth" from the ground. Then I retreated as gingerly as possible, ready at any moment to turn and run. I knew that I would be able to clear the barbed wire quickly and it would be a matter of whether I reached it before he reached me. He stood dazed for several moments and then backed away, much to my relief. Then he stood and pawed the ground. Not in the usual threatening manner of such animals, but in what I really believed was a gesture of appreciation. I was very relieved to cross the wire to safety, all the same.

St. Stephen's Day became, for Tommy and I, the traditional day for attending vermin shoots. Why that came about I do not know but it always seemed to suit our mood on the day. As soon as the dinner had been devoured we would be off to some wood or other and the afternoon would be spent cracking caps at pigeons, magpies and greycrows. I suppose the fact that pheasants were usually scarce at that time of year meant that we enjoyed the diversion. However, on one occasion I decided to take off with the dog for a ramble before lunch. I was feeling somewhat seedy after the celebrations of the previous days and felt the need for some fresh air. I had been walking for about an hour when I met a farmer who was well known to me. Jack Kelly was his name and, to my way of thinking, he was one of the good ones. He was carrying a billhook, which struck me as being somewhat odd, given the day that was in it. I assumed that he was going to lay a bush in a gap that was allowing cattle to escape onto the road.

He was always one for a chat so we spent the best part of an hour gabbing about one thing and another. He was leaning on the billhook, breastfeeding it as I would say, occasionally leaning back on his heels and using the hook to pick idly at pieces of grass, all the while telling me where he had seen pheasants in the previous weeks. In the manner of such discussions, one word borrowed another and, before I left, I inquired about the bit of fencing which had taken him from the fire on this of all days. His face was as straight as a widow's as he told me that there was no problem with the fences, but the bloody women had him damned for a bit of holly all over the Christmas. Not far from where we were standing, there was a beautiful tree of berried holly and I bit my lip hard to keep from laughing. I just wished that I could have been a fly on the wall in his kitchen when he arrived home to "undamn" himself. What, I wondered, would his wife and daughter say when he brought home holly at midday on St. Stephen's Day. That sheer harmless simplicity, from a man so well versed in the ways of the world, endeared him to me forever.

Another individual for whom I had the utmost respect was one Sean Quinn. A bachelor, he lived alone in a house which was about as remote as one would be likely to find in Co. Kilkenny. It seemed to us that the highlight of his year was when we came out for a shot and stopped to while away a few minutes. A shy, retiring man, he always appeared as though he would be happier if he could stand behind a wall to talk and not actually have to face people. He had a way of inclining his head away from whoever he was conversing with, which belied the fact that he was quite a good conversationalist and, had he been lucky in love, he might have made some woman very happy.

His business acumen was first rate and he ran his farm as competently as any. Yet he chose to live a fairly solitary lifestyle. His day would seem to brighten visibly when we arrived and he would talk about all the various birds and animals he would recently have seen. Depression may also have been a factor in his life, for the long winter evenings used to leave him feeling down. Frequently he would say to us that he had not been feeling all that well of late, to which we would invariably reply that "You must be over the worst of it now Sean. You're looking great. Never mind, once we get the Christmas and New Year over, you will begin to notice the stretch in the evenings and you'll be grand". This may sound patronizing, but it always seemed to be just what he needed to hear. Then he would bid us good luck and ramble about his business, chatting to his faithful Alsation dog.

Tommy, I would describe as a burlesque character, who had a natural talent for imitating the various mannerisms which people displayed. Needless to say he did this without intending any harm and to hear him telling stories about the said Sean was pure entertainment. I mention this simply as an introduction to an incident, which happened on the first of November, sometime back in the late eighties. Catch and myself had teamed up and were shooting, among other places, on Sean's land. Tommy and Paddy Dunne were elsewhere, all of us hoping to bag a specimen bird and take the trophy. We spotted Sean in the distance and changed course deliberately to talk to him. Partly because we knew that he would appreciate it and also because we felt he might point us in the right direction.

The discourse although brief, followed along pretty set lines. The weather was discussed and then the harvest and his state of health was commented on before we gently asked him how many birds he had seen of late. He mentioned having seen two good clutches all through the year and assured us that there were a fair number of cocks among them. Then he seemed to steady himself for a moment and told us about a sighting he had witnessed, sometime in June, while walking through a field of oats.

He had apparently been pulling weeds, which were scattered throughout the crop, when a strange bird flushed in front of him. This immediately caught our attention because in all the years we had known him, he had never been one for telling tall tales. As gently as we could, we prodded him for more information and in deadly serious tones he told us it was too big to be a pheasant. Then he went on, "by the way he flew straight across the field he would remind you of a bird that would be able to fly over the sea". At this stage we were beginning to reckon that he had been having hallucinations, but we still showed interest by asking what colour it had been. His face grimaced into a mask of confusion and, looking hard at his wellingtons he told us that "it was a kind of the colour of a car". Biting my lip has long been my way to keep myself from laughing in the wrong place and on this occasion I almost had to bite it clean off. We then queried the length of tail that this strange bird was sporting but he hadn't noticed, whereupon we parted with a promise to keep our eyes open and report any sightings and inform him of what it was. As we walked away we wondered just what he had been trying to describe by way of colour and could only guess that he was referring to a sort of metallic sheen. It was possibly a melanistic "black" cock, or even a green one which sometimes show up. Sometime later, we met with the other pair and, needless to say, the story lost nothing in the telling. Paddy Dunne was a noted wit and on hearing of this strange creature was fast in with a possible explanation, "bigger than a pheasant, the colour of a car with a long touring range, it could only have been one of those Flying Minibuses we keep hearing about". The number of times since then I have seen Tommy imitate Sean on that conversation is way beyond counting, but even though he was not there initially to hear it, he can still crease me up every time.

The author, in a world of his own.

CHAPTER SEVENTEEN

Throughout those years we had more fun times than I could ever hope to recount in a book of this nature and of course we had our share of harmless misfortune also. I believe it would have been about 1989 when I watched Tommy fall headlong into a drain on a Sunday morning in early January. Despite his discomfort, there was really nothing I could do, having pulled him out, except to laugh. We were hunting in somewhat unfamiliar territory and recent snow, which had been lying for some days, had suddenly melted and there was water just about everywhere. As we travelled we found that time after time we were forced to detour because drains, which were full to capacity, prevented us making any steady progress. Finally we approached one and, the long and the short of it was, that we either had to cross it or retrace our steps, all the way to the car. This was not an option for us, so I emptied my gun and gave it to him along with my bag and decided to jump.

I made a short run and reached the far side with nothing to spare. Although I was never the most athletic in the world I knew that I usually had the edge over Tommy in the long jump. In his younger days, he was an Irish champion boxer and was still quite fit but his short legs were built for power rather than distance. He then emptied his gun and offered them both across to me, together with the bags and his cartridge belt. As he walked away from the drain, I tried to tell him that there was really no need for a fifty-yard sprint but he wasn't having a bar of it. He took a couple of deep breaths and started with the kind of determination, which I had come to know so well, written all over his face. He was about two paces away from the edge when his foot slipped and suddenly his balance was lost and he was all over the place. He had far too much momentum to hope to stop so he ended up literally falling headlong in. His two arms, and all above them, was all that reached the bank where I was standing and all I did was to drag him out as quickly as I could. The cold of the water was something which I did not need telling about and, although my heart went out to him I really could not help laughing. I had suffered a somewhat similar fate the previous year, while shooting alone, and could not remember getting much sympathy from him. That story, incidentally, has already been published in a different forum so I cannot be said to be unfair.

There was one other occasion when his lack of prowess at jumping almost cost him very dearly indeed. We were hunting on the aforementioned Jack Kelly's land. Catch was with us on that occasion so it may well have been the first of November. I had temporarily parted from their company, while the dogs were working out a scent, and was about one hundred yards distant and did not see what happened. But according to Catch they were simply jumping a drain, which appeared straightforward enough. Catch jumped first, then somehow Tommy managed to get his foot entangled in the undergrowth as he leaped. To say that he fell awkwardly would be a serious understatement. He ended up crashing headlong into the far bank. In Catch's words, there was a sickening thud as his forehead made contact with the hard ground. For a very long moment, Catch thought that his neck was broken. The fright that Catch got stayed with him long after the fall affected the other fellow. I guess the training which he would have done on his neck muscles, to win an Irish title in the ring, stood him in good stead.

A psychologist might suggest that such memorable moments were instrumental in forming the great bond between Tommy and I, which has lasted so well for so many years. Perhaps this is so, but I reckon that there was so much more which can never really be quantified. The many long hours spent quietly waiting by countless duck-ponds, waiting for flighting mallard or teal, or standing at the edge of a wood in late winter and early spring, shooting pigeon on their way to roost. The many countless miles trudging wearily on, when the dogs failed to get a scent, probably because there wasn't any there although we might have thought different. The fact that neither of us had a greedy streak which meant that whenever the dog set we instinctively moved to cover all the options, regardless of who might get the shot. All of these things had their part to play. Then there were the endless evenings in Tommy's front room when, to the great amusement of his lovely wife Liz, we would recount the many strokes we pulled, whenever the need arose as it frequently did, to get the better of some individual who was less than happy to see us shoot for whatever reason. Also in that same front room we made plans for our next escapade or discussed such serious topics as the training of young dogs. I suppose at the end of the day it was the simple joy that we each derived from each other's company, which made it all so special.

The feeling and regard, which we had developed over the years, for our canine friends is something which should not go without mention. Two dogs of such different breeds do not always work well together.

We never encountered any real problems. They matured well, and taught us more about shooting than we ever taught them. I now believe that my Judy was the best dog which I have ever had the pleasure of shooting over. As the years went by, I regretted more and more the fact that I was so inexperienced when I bought her, that her training really left a lot to be desired. Many times I vowed, that if I lived long enough to try again with a pup, I would achieve much better results. Her natural ability and work-rate were beyond question but that tendency which she had to hunt for herself and expect me to simply follow on was not how I felt it should happen. That urge to try again was building inside me and once again I started reading that famous book in preparation. This time I felt that my experience should stand to me and, despite my great affinity for Judy, I was already looking forward to training her successor.

However there was much water to flow under many bridges before my time would come. In my youth, my Mother was known to caution me against wishing my life away, but as some great philosopher, whose name escapes me at the moment, once said, "the trouble with youth is that it is wasted on the young". For even before our eyes, great changes were taking place in the countryside and it seemed to be an almost daily whine of ours that some farm or other was being "cleaned up". The rate at which the cover was being erased was frightening and, long term, this would all have far reaching consequences for us.

Perhaps one of the most important points of all, from a field-sports perspective, was that between Tommy and myself we had reared three sons. My son Shane and Tommy's two lads Gregg and Thomas, together with their individual friends, were all encouraged at every opportunity to come along and enjoy the game. And for a time they did, but despite getting great fun from trudging the countryside in the wet and mud, and jumping drains and what have you, they never showed any real interest in carrying a gun. In fact they seemed somehow bemused by that side of things and really couldn't care less if we never got a shot. We never tried to push them, just simply hoped that one day the excitement would descend upon them rather like the Holy Ghost. Whether that was a mistake or not, will never be known, but at this stage it seems safe to say that the sport will die in our households with our passing. I have written about this also in another piece and it is worth saying that overall it is alarming to watch the decline in the numbers who appear to be taking up the sport. Catch and myself were discussing this problem over a pint in the not-too-distant past. Not counting Daddy's generation, we counted eleven shooting men whom we regarded as shooting partners at one time or another. Including ourselves that makes thirteen. The age range was from fifty-five down to forty. Only ourselves and one other still follow a gun. Even more alarming is the statistic that those thirteen men reared twenty-two sons between them. Of those, only one took shooting seriously and I believe he still does.

It might be very interesting, if depressing, to do a poll in any number of national schools around the country. I am talking about rural schools here, just to see what would be the average reaction to the idea of banning field-sports entirely. I am aware that the N.A.R.G.C. are working with teachers to promote a more enlightened view of hunting in general, but I wonder if it is too little, too late.

CHAPTER EIGHTEEN

The summer of 1989 is one I will long remember as being the time when I fell into bad company and was lured from the straight and narrow path which I had always tried to follow. I was on what should have been an innocuous holiday with my wife. Being people of simple tastes, we were touring along the Western seaboard and staying, as the fancy took us, in Bed and Breakfast accommodation. I shall refrain from further identifying the town in question, for reasons which shall become apparent. We spent a couple of nights in a delightful house and, by pure chance, when we visited the local hostelry we actually found ourselves sitting with the couple who owned the house where we were staying.

One word borrowed another as often happens and as the night wore merrily on, I found myself and the man, whom I shall call Pierce, chatting fondly about our mutual love of fishing among other things. The two ladies were engaged in much more serious matters and, as is my wont, I quietly recited my own poem: "Ode to the Anti's". Pierce listened with the greatest of attention and, after making me feel suitably proud of my poetic endeavours, he said quietly,"if you ever want material for more poetry, I've got just the thing". Not sure if the alcohol was having more serious effect, than I would have expected, on a man of his age and size, I was about to ignore the comment when he continued. "I can show you the most poetic method of removing a salmon from the water that you ever imagined". At this stage he had my undivided attention and I listened intently as he spoke lovingly about, what was for him, an all-consuming passion in life. The long and short of it was, that he promised that if I was prepared to leave my bed at three forty-five a.m., he would take me on a little jaunt. My wife, when she heard about the plan a little later, was convinced that I had finally flipped, but I was on holiday and nothing was going to stop me.

At three-fifty a.m. there was a light knock on the bedroom door and I was already dressed at that stage. From a shed at the back, Pierce fitted me with a pair of oversized wellingtons and an old shooting jacket. Similarly attired himself, he threw a pair of chest waders over his shoulder and, picking up a rather odd-shaped landing net, he headed off with me in tow down a small boreen that led from the back of his house to a river some five hundred yards distant.

It was a dull misty dawn as we made our way down and the fact that I might, at any minute, be arrested did little to dissuade me from the mission. I could always claim that I was only there to watch.

As we approached the river, the sound of water rushing headlong over a weir grew louder. We slipped quietly through a well-worn hole in a hedge and he stepped cautiously forward to check over a wall to make sure that we were the only individuals around. Then we quickly descended a set of steel steps and were soon concealed between the wall and some overhanging branches. Immediately in front of us the river roared on its merry way to the sea. The weir was a perfect V shape with the water flowing from our left, cascading down over the V, in a fall of about three feet to what appeared to be a flat bed of concrete. From there, it ran for another eight or ten feet and tumbled in a raging, white foam, into a deep hole, which seemed to me to be capable of sucking the unwary to eternity.

As we stood, I noticed that his eyes were moving

at all times. Checking the far side of the river, left and right, then over his shoulder, while at the same time closely watching the swirling water at the hole for sign of a fish. This, he told me, was all-important. "You must see the fish before he begins to make his run. Otherwise you will be too late".

The rather large landing net was triangular in shape with the broad end farthest away and with a fairly short handle of about four feet. When the fish starts to run, he explained, you have to move quickly. "If he gets over the weir he is gone and there is nothing you can do about it. But sometimes he fails to get up and tumbles back helplessly into the deep water. It is at that stage that I hope to take him". Looking at the current, I thought that he was off his rocker but since I was only there to watch and not actually put myself at risk I was happy enough. Suddenly he was gone and in an instant he was moving rather precariously across the "flat water", towards the far side of the V. I just had time to see the fish as he ploughed his way up the last foot of the climb and disappeared over the top. Untroubled, Pierce returned and said simply that luck was not always on your side.

The excitement which I was experiencing was as good as anything that I had known before in pursuit of game, no doubt partly because of the fear of getting caught. The minutes dragged by slowly and in the blink of an eye he was gone again. This time the fish failed to make the weir and as he tumbled back I felt sure that he was in the bag. However, as he was falling backwards, he managed to give a mighty splash of his tail which sent him scurrying across at an angle and past the waiting net to freedom. This time I began to wonder if this method of fishing was worth the risk involved, considering the returns. The thought had only just entered my head when another fish ran. Pierce was back on the run instantly and, just as quickly, he was back with the fish jumping and struggling for all he was worth in the net. He handed me the net telling me to hold him and as I did so I was struck by the awesome power of the animal.

Remember, this was the first time I had seen a salmon, outside a fishmongers, and this one was not played out on the end of a rod and line. He was completely fresh and about eight pounds weight. It was now five-thirty a. m. and he decided that we only had until six. Desperately, I wanted to see another fish caught and twice more I saw Pierce run and each time he came back empty-handed, as the fish cleared the obstacle and was gone. With one minute to go before we were due to leave, another fish ran almost beside where we were standing and where I had not been looking all morning. Pierce however was on the ball and in a flash there were two fish in the bag. It was killed with the same calm efficiency as the first. Then, with not a hint of furtiveness about his movements, he picked up the first fish and placed it in the net alongside the second and strode purposefully home.

At six-fifteen there was a mighty smell of frying bacon in the kitchen and we had a royal breakfast together before the rest of the house stirred. Among the stories he told, and he had a penchant for them, was of a day some two years previous when he almost drowned. It was a morning just like the one we had just enjoyed, except that the river was running high after recent rain. When he arrived at his station he decided right off that the flow of water was too strong for comfort and it would be, not just unwise but unsafe, to follow a fish. However, as a lover of solitude and the sound of the weir and the dawn chorus, he decided to stand and watch awhile.

After fifteen minutes he had witnessed five fish running and not one of them made it over and his teeth were watering at the chances which he was missing. Suddenly a fish ran and he knew right away that this was the fish of a lifetime. The sheer mass of the fish was evident even in the unusually high water and man's oldest enemy, greed, overcame his natural caution. He lifted the net and went across, struggling to maintain his balance in the current, which was more than knee-high. Caring nothing for the foamy spray which was hitting his midriff, he followed the fish to where it started to climb and watched the fierce struggle which it made as he held the net in position. He hoped against all hope to see him fail and tumble back to the waiting net. With a final swish of his mighty tail, the fish scaled the weir and was gone. He gave a sort of reverent salute as he turned just a little carelessly and lost his balance.

His attempt to shout was cut off in an instant, as he took a lung-full of water and was sucked, head first, into the swirling black hole which he had for so long feared might one day be his end. He remembers being tossed about and slammed against several rocks, losing consciousness for a time. The next thing he remembers is feeling himself pushing against the bank and reaching up and grabbing an overhanging branch. He managed to hold on to it, but it was several moments of gasping for breath and coughing water, before he was able to clearly identify his situation. Then, with his chest waders carrying a lot of water, he had an almighty struggle to pull himself up the bank to safety.

Fortunately he was on the home side of the river, although this was entirely due to good fortune and he was almost home before the extreme cold hit him. The oil burner from his central heating system was in his garage and he just sat there to dry off and contemplate what might have been. He was able to laugh about it as he told me, but he was very willing to admit that the incident had a very real and lasting effect.

About a month later, Catch and myself journeyed to see him and stayed over for the chance of an early morning expedition. On that, and several subsequent occasions, we quietly watched that man ply his trade and agreed without question that he was pure poetry in motion. The man may come across as a simple poacher to many, but knowing him and his method, we would agree entirely that he would kill no more fish than a reasonably competent rod angler. The fish he was taking were in the whole of their health, unlike the despicable practice we know happens where fish are lifted with the aid of a lamp and a gaff from the spawning redds. In his own sweet way, he gave as much time and patience to his sport as a legitimate angler and got just as much pleasure. I know I certainly did. When I recited for him the poem, which his game had inspired me to write he was suitably impressed and he now has a framed copy hanging in his hallway. There are two things which I must make clear here. Neither Catch nor myself ever actually participated in this awful crime. We were there for research purposes only and I have no doubt that the world will believe that, given our record. The second is that the rack and thumbscrews would not make me divulge where it all took place. I assured Pierce that I would never besmirch his name, but rather enshrine it forever in poaching lore.

In the days that followed I was haunted by that mighty fish, and the means of catching him. This poem, I hope, captures the essence of the story.

Yours truly with my first ever fresh salmon.

THE SALMON THAT FAILS TO GET UP

Mother Nature can be difficult, on that we all agree,
The Rabbit gets the Mixi, the Badger gets TB,
The Whales get stuck in the Arctic ice and Seals will die with the
flu,
But the Salmon's biggest problem is the Bould 'O Murachu'.

Come all you city slickers who boast you've been around,
And hear a fishy story from a little western town,
About a man called 'Murphy' who likes to drink a sup,
And who spends his mornings waiting, for the salmon that fails to
get up.

Like the Heron, quiet and deadly, he stands behind a wall,
His eyes are fixed unerringly on the spot where the waters fall,
For an hour he stands unmoving, then suddenly there's a rush of
spray,
As a salmon goes up and over the weir. He's the one that got away,
But as the Heron returns to the darkness to watch and wait once
more,
His patience is scarcely ruffled, for he's seen it all before.

And while the dawn is breaking over a city that's still asleep,
The Heron's eyes are fixed again on the white water over the deep,
When suddenly another fish runs, the man tiptoes over the black,
But this fish fails to make it, and this time there's no way back,
For he's in the net and jumping like many a fish before,
As the Heron returns to the darkness, to watch and wait once more.

As he does his priestly duties and the salmon is laid to rest,
He thinks again of the days long gone, when the fishing was at its best,
And as his mind will wander, so better those days will seem,
As he remembers the thirty-pounders, now few and far between.

Later in the local, he'll quietly sit and say,
I bagged three fish this morning 'Catch', but the big one got away,
And 'Catch' just sits there knowingly, and quietly drinks his sup,
For he too knows the thrill of waiting, for the Salmon that fails to
get up.

So let the Conservationist argue, that the Salmon was born to go,
That the bailiff is his greatest friend on earth and the poacher his
deadliest foe,
They'll point to the thirty-pounders and tell us the reason they've
gone,
Has nothing to do with Nature, but the Heron who fishes at dawn.

But there's another story I've never told as yet,
About the men who poach the seas, with the monofilament net,
But down here in the local, the lads all feel the same,
To outsiders this might be poaching, but to us it's purely a game.

Let me finally offer a challenge, to those who cannot agree,
Why not come down to this man's town and have a drink on me,
You can leave behind the cheque-book and bring along the wife,
And we'll sit and spin a merry tale on the simple things in life.

For I can tell a story, I have travelled far and near,
I've chased the big fish in the deep, I've hunted highland deer,
I can talk about the fishing on Corrib, Mask and Conn,
I've hunted pheasants on the flat, and grouse on Sliabh na mBan.
But I will back my promise, and I'll pay for whatever we sup,
If you can tell me what's better than waiting, for the Salmon that
fails to get up.

by Martin Grennan.

CHAPTER NINETEEN

When I returned home, after seeing that first fish being caught, I was aware of a need inside me which had not really troubled me before. Tommy was as excited when he heard the story, as I had been, and resolved then and there to see this magic in action. His time did not come until two years later. In the meantime I was bubbling with excitement at the memory of that magnificent fish. Heretofore I had only known the power of a trout. But having felt the power of that perfectly fresh run salmon I just knew that somehow I had to get one on the end of a line. It was nearing the end of the summer at this stage and the only thing which we knew about salmon angling was, that the season started on the first of February and ended on the thirtieth of September. So we decided that it was not worth buying a licence for the remainder of the year, given that we had yet to equip ourselves with gear. So, another shooting season was to come and go before we would tackle this latest craze.

When the time finally arrived, on a frosty Sunday morning in February, we were equipped with all the necessary gear and what little knowledge we had been able to glean from books in the meantime. We decided to start at the top of our beat and fish downstream. We had shiny new rods and reels, the finest of line, baits and a net which was big enough to land anything that the river Nore could throw at us. After the hard slog of recent Sundays tramping the countryside in search of pheasants, the fishing was something of a dawdle. I suppose we had been casting, more in hope than expectation, for about half an hour when a fish suddenly leaped two feet clear of the water just in front of Tommy. The level of excitement, which this created, was indescribable. Suddenly we knew we were in the right area, which of course was all due to good judgement. We felt that catching a fish was now merely a formality. For the next two hours we fished with total concentration. Then, just as our spirits started to flag, there was another mighty splash and again we fished on with confidence. At the end of the session we were still fishless but happy. We ranted and raved about it throughout the week and were back on the bank the following Sunday morning, determined as ever.

It was about eleven a.m. when Tommy gave a shout. I was about thirty yards downstream when I heard him and I looked back to see his rod bent double. There was no mistaking the cause of the tremor in his voice. I reeled in my own line and ran back, preparing the net as I went. The fish was struggling about a foot beneath the surface, clearly visible. The clutch on the reel was whining every few seconds, from the pressure which Tommy was exerting on him. Suddenly the fish took off across the river towards where we could see a partially submerged branch of a tree and for one awful moment we thought that he would snag the line. But his run stopped just short of the danger area and he gave in to the pull which he was feeling and headed back towards where we were standing. At this stage I was lying at right angles to the river, with the net already in the water and as the fish came like a torpedo I just waited and let him swim straight in. Then I lifted him clear of the water and moved back, lest he should somehow jump free of the net.

He displayed pretty much the same level of strength as the fish which I had seen Pierce snatch, even though he had been forced to tire himself out in the struggle. As soon as I had laid him to rest I reached to shake Tommy's hand and knew that the smile on his face could only be a mirror image of my own. For several minutes we just stood around admiring him and enjoying the feeling of accomplishment. Then I suddenly remembered having read that salmon are gregarious and that whenever a fish is caught there is usually another close by. We fished on with renewed vigour and the birds in the trees seemed to be happy for us. Some twenty minutes later I felt a tug and the process started all over again with me fighting, as though for my life, and Tommy wielding the net. Again, he was landed safely, almost like a twin of the first. They were both like bars of silver and about six or seven pounds weight. We decided it was time to quit and go for a drink. These things do not happen every day, so a celebration was well in order.

On the drive back to town, I remarked to Tommy that I was somewhat disappointed with the short length of time which it had taken to land both fish. He was in full agreement, once I had voiced the opinion, so we decided that they had probably run straight in from the sea and we were unlucky to catch them at their lowest ebb. That settled any doubts which we had and so, two very proud anglers entered the pub still full to overflowing with all the joys of spring. I suppose it was fate that did it, but for whatever reason, my ould mate Johnny Meany was in situ at the counter, just inside the door. For the next ten minutes he listened to our tale, with something of a bemused smile on his face, and then very gently tried to explain the facts of life to us-at least those that pertain to salmon angling. Or to put it in Biblical terms, The Truth unto us was shown. Those two beautiful fish were spent. Their proper name being Kelts. That is to say that they had already successfully made the return journey to their spawning ground and were now on the way back to salt water.

To prove the point, he came out to the car to inspect the fish and ran his finger along the flank of each fish in turn, pointing out to us the slackness in the belly, and also the way in which the vent was extruded in both carcasses. He was, however, sympathetic to our feelings and assured us that, when our turn came as it surely would, that we would know immediately the difference between this and the real thing. Whereupon, we returned to the bar and drank to the good health of the two dead fish. During the next couple of hours there was a lot of lighthearted banter and slagging but, in the midst of it all, Johnny imparted some valuable advice about salmon fishing which was to stand me in good stead in the future.

In simple terms he told me the name of a book called "Salmon Fishing. A practical guide" by Hugh Falkus. That book, although not cheap, was worth every penny. I read it from cover to cover on at least three occasions and still pick it up every now and then to read certain passages and never fail to learn something new. There is simply a wealth of experience and an understanding of the philosophy of salmon angling which has enriched every occasion on which I have since set forth. In the meantime, Tommy and I carried on fishing throughout that spring. Over the next couple of Sundays we met and released several more of those spent fish until finally a flood came which left the river unfishable for about three weeks, after which the Kelts had all been safely taken back to sea and the river was left fresh and clean for the next run.

The run of Spring fish had all but dried up in the river Nore and so it was late May before we started to hear of fresh fish being caught. The summer run tends to be "grilse" in the main, which are small fish of about four to six pounds weight, having spent only one winter at sea. The occasional full grown salmon comes with them but the main run of heavy fish comes in the Autumn. It was mid-June before a shout went up from Tommy. We were flogging the water, which was in peak condition after a spate and somehow I was not surprised despite the length of time we had been waiting. I was following downstream and looked up, to see the fish in midair, in a spectacular leap and I was at Tommy's side in an instant. The fight lasted for about five or six minutes and during that time, I doubt if either of us caught too many breaths. He was leaping about all over the place and alternately running upstream and down. Twice he came close to the net but swam doggedly away each time before finally turning on his side in midstream, from where he was carefully guided towards the waiting net and carried quickly ashore.

After I had done my priestly duty I shook Tommy's hand and the happy smile on his face is something I will not forget. Once again, we backed up and fished down the same stretch of water and twenty minutes later Tommy was into a fish again. When he was landed he looked like a slightly bigger brother to the first and when we weighed them later, they weighed five and a half, and six pounds respectively. Tommy openly lamented the fact that I had not struck lucky but I knew my time would come. For now, I was simply basking in reflected glory and advising all and sundry that he had fished exactly the way I had taught him.

Two days later, I felt the first tug of a fish and for about ten minutes I endured torture, waiting for the line to snap or the hook to pull free, but I won the battle in the end and landed a magnificent ten and a half pound fish. To be honest, I was surprised at just how good the feeling was. I laid him on the grass, and after the regulation handshake with my auld partner, I just sat down and admired the prize. After many minutes, I decided to fish on but my concentration kept wandering back to where the fish was lying and after half an hour we gave up and headed for home. As I walked up the bank, with the rod in one hand and the fish hanging by the tail in the other, I was remembering the time long ago when I proudly carried home my first rabbit and the small boy was jumping about inside me once again. In a euphoric flight of fancy, I remembered the stories from my childhood about the Great Kings of Ireland and the Fianna and how they used to hunt the mighty Red Deer, and the great banquets which followed. I wanted to keep on walking right up to the King's Castle and lay the fish on the table and tell the servant, "Have your best man prepare this for the table. Then bring silver goblets of your finest claret wine for the King and I, for the hunter has returned and I must tell the King a tale".

CHAPTER TWENTY

For Tommy and myself, the passing years were marked most clearly by the changing face of the countryside. Season after season saw the destruction of more and more game habitat as more and more hedgerows were cleared to accommodate machinery. Several farms were bulldozed into single fields and in many instances the ditches which remained were cut to the quick. But an even more immediate problem was catching up with us, which we scarcely noticed. Those two dogs, which had given so much service, were aging and showing all the signs of slowing down. In the end, the springer was first to go although that was due to a tragedy beyond anyone's control.

The dog was playing with some of the local children when another dog arrived on the scene and a fight developed. Unfortunately, a young lad of about seven or eight tried to intervene and ended up getting scratched in the process. He came away crying that Judy had bitten him. This was most unlikely and totally unprovable, but Tommy and his family felt that they could not expect the child to live and play happily on the street with the dog, which he believed had bitten him. Reluctantly they took the hard decision to have her put down. For what it's worth I believe they were right.

Whether or which, Tommy was in a somewhat distressed state when he phoned to ask me to take the dog to the vet. I agreed and arrived at his house that evening to find that he had gone for a walk. Liz and I then put the dog in the car and made the short drive across town. The number of times when I had taken that little springer for a drive is beyond counting. Yet, when I attempted to put the lead on and take her out at the vet's office she tried to evade me and run off. I quieted her down and walked her in, although she was somewhat reticent. The procedure took but a few minutes and we were both glad that we could take the remains out through a side door, away from the gaze of people in the waiting room. No matter how it is done, it is never a pleasant experience and Liz was visibly upset.

We then drove to Desart wood, a place where Judy would have been very familiar with, to bury her. I had brought a shovel and spade but no pick. The ground was rock hard and Liz laughed a little as I struggled. When the job was complete, I walked around until I found a good size stone and placed it at the head of the grave. That done, we drove home, found Tommy and went for a drink. For the remainder of the evening, we reminisced and wondered how long it would be before the second half of that chapter would be closed. The pointer had been neutered some years previously and had tended to carry a lot of weight as a result. This situation was not helped by the kindness of two old ladies who had a penchant for buying sweet cakes for her on their daily trips to town. Several times I tried to put her on a strict diet and exercise routine but the effort was becoming just too much for her.

As the summer turned to autumn we realized that we were going to have to replace the springer. All the usual adverts were scanned and finally, on the eve of the new shooting season, Tommy phoned and asked if I would go with him to buy a pup. Catch had arrived in readiness for the following morning, so all three of us set off on a drive of about twelve miles. He had heard of Llewllyn setter pups for sale and, as soon as we drove into the farmyard, we were met by two of the finest setters I have ever seen. I think all three of us decided immediately that any offspring of those would have to be worth buying. In the event there were only two pups remaining from a litter of eight. One dog, one bitch. Tommy's intention was to buy the male, but for whatever reason, the bitch kept pulling at his shoelaces and he was smitten. I personally would not have bought a bitch but when I realized that the dog was there for the taking I decided on the spot to buy him as well.

There was a certain amount of alcohol consumed thereafter and I can fairly say that our hopes and aspirations were at an all time high for the future of our sport. As for me, I was filled with anticipation, for the possibilities which were suddenly before me. Earlier that afternoon I had not the slightest notion of buying a pup and now I was the proud owner of what I felt must be a distant descendant of the dog of my early days. Before the pup reached home I had named him Grouse, like his forefather. But I was determined that he would not grow to be bold. This dog would be trained to perfection.

The following morning was, what is often called the morning after the night before, and we were slow off the mark. Rather unusual for us on November the first, but it was in keeping with Judy. She was only able, at this stage, to put her front paws into the boot of the car and had to be lifted in. She hunted gamely for the first half of the day and we shot a couple of cocks before dinner. We gave her an extended break, in the hope that she might be able to finish the day, but for the first time ever we were in the car and heading home before four o' clock. The atmosphere in the car was a strange mixture of sadness and excitement. We couldn't help looking forward to great times which we felt were just ahead, but at the same time we realized that it was going to be very difficult to ever replace the two Judys. They had given great service and my heart was heavy with the knowledge that I would soon have a very unpleasant task to attend to.

For the rest of that season, we were restricted to shooting for just a half day at a time and even that became just a gentle ramble for Judy and myself on occasions. At times, she would get so tired that she seemed distracted and would amble over to a bunch of nettles and set, more in hope than expectation. In ways it was comical to watch but she would still show signs of excitement as soon as she saw me produce the gun. In the meantime, the pup was taking all my spare time. The book had given me something of an insight into the business of forming a relationship with a dog and, for the first three months I just played with him every chance I got, and gradually got him to the stage where he felt comfortable on the lead. Teaching him to come to his name was child's-play, with the aid of his food dish, and from then on I just let him enjoy being a pup. Probably the worst thing which you can do to a dog is to expect him to learn too much too soon. I was totally determined that I was not going to lose my temper at any stage. The confidence which a dog develops, can be shattered by a harsh telling off, particularly if he is unsure of what he has done wrong. Fortunately my job at that time allowed me to get home during the day for short spells and I was able to play with him for about ten or fifteen minutes at a stretch, two or three times daily.

The last day of that season was a Saturday and I

decided to take a stroll with the pointer. Although I carried the gun, I had little real expectation of getting a shot. Birds at that stage are about as scarce as hens' teeth. It was a pleasant afternoon and she set early on and flushed a hen, which excited and disappointed me at the same time. After that she started into her little game of setting into bunches of nettles without producing anything. Then as we approached a copse of trees she appeared to pick up a scent and followed a trail for about thirty yards before setting dead. I knew that my chances of getting a clear shot at whatever might flush were slim, but I hoped for all I was worth that it would be a cock. There was about one very tense minute of absolute silence and suddenly a cock broke cover, crowing at full blast and moving through the trees in a flash. I fired one quick shot and hit him hard. He dropped a leg and swayed heavily but managed to stay airborne and disappeared from view. I cursed myself for not killing him cleanly and set about following him. We hunted several ditches without a trace and in the end I decided to give up.

It was starting to get dark so we headed in the direction of the car and were less than one hundred yards away when Judy set suddenly into a drain. Then, without any command from me, she plunged into the undergrowth and came out with the bird in her mouth, dropping it at my feet. He was dead where he landed. Judy had always been good on a wounded bird, but somehow I knew that this particular find would live in my memory for many years to come. I bagged the bird and patted her warmly and we plodded our way back to the car, knowing that she would not make it to another season.

In shooting circles, there has long raged a debate

about the proper way to end a dog's life. Some people insist that they should be allowed to die naturally like humans. Others believe that it is a job for a vet and would have no time whatever for the idea of shooting a dog. This had been Tommy's way and I know he had doubted that, when push would come to shove, I would be any different. But I come from the school which believes, that if it is my dog, then it is my job. Throughout the spring of that year Judy became more and more uncomfortable and finally, in early May, I decided the time had come. My heart was heavy as I took the gun from the press and took her from her pen. Gamely, she put her front paws into the boot and when I had lifted her in, I drove once more to Desart Wood.

As we left the car she seemed totally contented and ambled along almost aimlessly. When I stopped beside an oak tree she simply laid down and a moment later it was all over. The sudden silence, which followed the loud report, was awesome. It reminded me of the time so long ago when Daddy had shot the jackdaws, which had so tormented my poor Mother. After a long moment I emptied the gun and returned it, broken and open, to the car.

This time I had a pick to hand, but did not need it, as the ground had not yet dried up to any great extent. Again I dug a shallow grave and, having back-filled it, I found a suitable sized stone and marked the spot. I was not in much form for company, so for the next two hours, I simply walked around the wood, thinking back and gradually I found words starting to take some kind of shape in my head. I know many people will think that I am heartless and some have openly told me so. Be that as it may, I will offer here the poem, which I composed in my head, as I walked.

A FRIEND IS GONE

'Tis hard to tell a story spanning almost seven years
To remember all the good times and still hold back the tears
For my faithful pointer Judy at last has reached the end
Having earned herself the title - A Shooting Man's Best Friend.

With my shooting partner Tommy and his little Springer bitch
We had a dog to range the stubbles and a dog to hunt the ditch
Far over heather-mountain and over grassland bare
We hunted grouse and pheasant behind that faithful pair.

But alas in early summer, a chill runs through my blood
As I make that fateful journey to the heart of Desart Wood
My throat is dry and lumpy, my heart is sad and sore
For it was here we laid the Springer down, not yet a year before.

The woods are strangely silent, the birds make not a sound
As Judy, now too tired to hunt, lies peaceful on the ground
My eyes are dim and misty, my hands are all a-quiver
'Tis so unjust, but still I must, that fatal shot deliver.

Alas, the deed is over, her very all she gave
So for her best endeavours I dig a shallow grave
And just to mark her resting-place, I find a single stone
My heart, like my gun, is broken, on the lonely walk back home.

by Martin Grennan.

CHAPTER TWENTY-ONE

I can honestly say that, throughout that Spring, I was having a ball. Grouse, while still only a pup, was maturing into a carbon copy of the dog we had seen, on the night I bought him. To say that he was spirited would be a serious understatement. At six months old, about the end of February, he was what the book described as hand-trained. That is to say, that he knew and responded to his name, and walked nicely on the lead and sat when I stopped and remained there, for ever longer periods of time. The trouble only started when he learned that, as soon as the lead came off, he was free to run. This was fine, until he got his first smell and took off in pursuit of whatever had caused it. Suddenly, his name was forgotten and the "Devil or Doctor Foster" would not bring him back until he grew tired of the hunt and came floundering back, breathless.

Like the good book suggested, I sat him down and spoke sternly to him. I left him sitting there until I felt the lesson had been learned and five minutes later we were back where we started with him running about the place and me on the verge of giving up. Then I introduced the whistle, giving it a long sharp blast immediately before calling his name and after only a couple of tries, I noticed him responding to the sound. Then I started to give it two short blows before commanding him to sit and, in almost no time, he was quite proficient at sitting to the whistle alone. Then when we were out for a ramble, he picked up a bone and I became frightened in case it might be poisoned, and shouted at him to drop it. Of course he did not understand the command as he had not heard it previously and when I rushed to take it from him he started running round in circles. Fortunately, the book had advised strongly against ever chasing a dog for something because he then regards the chase as a game, and one which he will win easily. So instead I just walked away and, in alarm, he came to me. That simple little success was enough to prove a very important point in the book, that a human being is infinitely more intelligent than a dog and, any problem encountered while training, can be overcome with a little thought.

As he grew, both in stature and confidence, he began to show some of the wildness for which Llewllyns are famous, at least those that I have known. The dog of my childhood had been totally untrained and, on a couple of occasions when this one got beyond a certain distance-about eighty yards-he soon realized that he was free to do as he pleased. He would race across distant meadows, with his ears and tail streaming backwards, and on several occasions I was left sitting in the middle of a field with nothing to do but wait for his return. At such times I would use the time to try to calm myself lest I should do something too drastic when he came back. A stern telling off is really all that is of any use. When he first encountered cattle, he was not the least impressed. The heavy bullocks were curious and came crowding around for a closer look. Grouse took one look and raced for the nearest hole in a hedge, through which he could escape. Then, he made his way back to the car, where I found him some minutes later, shivering in terror. I patted and coaxed him and we made friends and ended the lesson.

On the next occasion when I took him out, it was to a field containing about a dozen suck-calves. I kept him on the lead and, as the calves approached, I made him sit and hunkered down beside him. I soothed and stroked him and let the calves come in close and then shooed them away. Gradually, I started to walk him along on the lead, pushing the animals ahead of us and after a few minutes his confidence came soaring back. After that it was a simple step up to the bigger cattle, repeating the procedure, and ever after he was able to run rings round them. The full value of this lesson was often obvious in later years when I worked with grown dogs that had never learned not to be afraid of cattle. A tiresome problem, to put it mildly.

Water was another problem for him. What few drains we encountered had only low levels, and although I made a point of splashing about noisily, he refused to have anything to do with them and simply skipped over them. That was, until one day when we were walking along the bank of a fair sized river, and I noticed him getting excited as he picked up a trail.

Prior to this, he had only ever trailed rabbits, with quite a few sets on larks, but this was different. Suddenly he froze in a perfect point, which lasted all of about five seconds, until a hen pheasant flushed right from under his nose and flew straight across the river. The shock of the sudden appearance of the bird seemed to stun him momentarily and then he plunged headlong into the water and was out the far side before he knew what had happened. He followed the departing hen to the far end of the field before giving up the chase and came bounding back, once more crossing the river without batting an eyelid. From that moment, he had no further problem, although not being a retriever he never really seemed to develop a liking for water.

I should point out that Tommy was also having great success with his bitch, Sally. By and large they were trained separately because of different work schedules, so on the occasions when we did get together it was a real thrill to see how the two dogs liked to lose the run of themselves initially. For the first few minutes, they would be all over each other and then we would walk in separate directions and start to work the dogs as individuals. Then we would each command the dogs to quarter different sides of the field for a few minutes and then swap them over. In this way we were strengthening the level of control which we had over them, and also checking the possibility that either dog was failing to find game. By the time the following season came around they were about fifteen months old. Although the good book did not recommend shooting over dogs until they were at least two years old, we were totally dependant on them at this stage and were not about to lose another shooting season. When at last the first of November arrived, we set out with hope and aspirations at an all time high. Catch was with us, as usual for the first day, and I think he believed I had flipped my lid when I told him that in the event of Grouse setting that he was welcome to take the shot, because I wanted to concentrate on handling the dog.

As it transpired, the first set was in a wet grassy field and I knew instinctively that it was a snipe. The dog worked to perfection and when the little bird flushed I shot him cleanly. I felt the omens were good. By the end of the day we had shot four cocks, with both dogs performing relatively well. To say that we were happy would be a serious understatement. All the months of hard work and preparation was suddenly coming to fruition and the future looked exceedingly bright. Those dogs were well and truly "Toasted" in a certain hostelry that night, but nobody took any cognizance of the fact that those were young birds and that the cover at that time of year was heavy. Rather later in the season they began to give cause for concern when they started to flush birds prematurely, especially when the cover was light and they seemed to know instinctively where a cock was lying. Also, when ranging across stubbles they tended to run at a frantic pace and run right into a bird without scenting it until it was airborne. This was a very frustrating problem, for which the book recommended a couple of solutions, none of which worked to any great degree. Whether it was incompetence on the part of the trainers, or a lack of natural instinct and ability in the dogs, is open to conjecture. Personally I believe it was the latter. In any case, by the end of the season we were feeling slightly dejected but still hopeful, that age and experience would do the trick. It may sound strange but it is difficult to sort out these kind of problems during the closed season and somehow the following season crept in and the trouble was by now even more pronounced.

The following two years were to prove very frustrating for both Tommy and myself. The destruction of game habitat continued apace and it seemed that every day we went out we saw the damage being done by machinery. This was something which was particularly close to Tommy's heart and he was forever vocal about it. Insurance had become a big issue in our area also, due to a somewhat unfortunate accident, which resulted in a claim being lodged against a farmer and corresponding bad feeling. I don't wish to comment on a particular case, but in general I always felt that anyone who injured themselves while out shooting should expect no compensation from a landowner. In time, the insurance issue was resolved, pretty much to everybody's satisfaction, but a lot of harm had been done in the meantime. I believe that a lot of the hype was caused by both the insurance companies and the solicitors. They were, as usual, the ones with the most to gain from any controversy.

Along the way, we had more than our fair share of run-ins with farmers who probably had just cause for concern. Those two problems, together with the fact that the two dogs which we had worked so hard to train were not performing like we had hoped meant that it was all becoming too much. Now, more and more, as we walked we allowed our thoughts to turn to the very real problem of what we would do with our time whenever we gave up shooting. For a time, the real interest seemed to have waned and, all too often, we would walk halfheartedly and end up just leaning on a gate, instead of crossing it, wondering if old age was the real culprit. Still I believed that the sport had a lot to offer if the dogs were replaced. Not a pleasant thought, given that dogs are pets as well as working animals and certain little people become very attached to them. At the end of the third season I had had enough. Too often in the months of December and January, I had spoken to shooters who were bemoaning the fact that there were no birds left, while I was seeing several every time I went out. The problem was that the dog was flushing them way out of range and consequently they were still there the next day. At the end of that season, I did a lot of soul searching and decided to bite the bullet.

The first thing I did was I decided that I wanted to

try shooting over a Labrador and, having made my mind up, I promptly sold the Llewllyn. Then I set about finding a replacement and, after a short search, I found what I was looking for.

Full of excitement, Tommy and myself drove about seventy miles one lovely spring morning and looked at a beautiful litter of pups. Black, Golden and Chocolate, we were spoilt for choice and for nearly an hour we watched them playing about the yard and frolicking with us, trying to decide which one I should take. Finally, by some coincidence, we both were taken by the same black dog. On the road home, I named him Sherlock, after the great detective. After all, this thing was going to have to sniff out clues and find and retrieve game, so the name seemed to fit. There followed the usual amount of getting to know him, and hand training and starting to train him properly, and then I began to notice that something was not quite right. Puppies are, by their very nature, full of energy and fun. This little fellow seemed to have something less than half a tankful. He would play for ten minutes and then fall asleep for a couple of hours at a time. Then, when I would throw a dummy and send him to retrieve, he would gallop away excitedly and pick it up. But instead of returning it to hand, he would lie down and rest. I contacted the Vet, who was as concerned as I was and wanted to see the dog for herself.

After seeing the dog performing, or rather not, she decided to do some blood tests for analysis. Those first tests proved nothing and by now, even the vet was perplexed. She spoke to some colleagues in her practice and still could not come up with a solution. More tests were tried, without success, and finally they sought the help of a vet who had more experience of treating pets, rather than farm animals. This time, the answer came quickly. The dog had a condition called "Hip Displacia". This is a problem where the hip joints are not growing properly and, the long and the short of it was, that this pup had no future as a working dog. When I broke the news to Tommy he was very downbeat. This meant that another season was nearly upon us and still we had no dog. We went for a pint and discussed the various possibilities and finally he proffered his hand and said, "Martin, I've had enough. I'm going to take up golf". Thereafter, we had a lot of pints but nothing I could say would make him change his mind. The shooting partnership was over, but fortunately the friendship continues to the present day.

Front cover. Dog tired and contented.

CHAPTER TWENTY TWO

As the season approached, I acquired a dog of somewhat doubtful parentage and had just about enough time to get to know him before November the first. He was four years old and had never been trained. Consequently, we never really worked as a team, nonetheless we shot a decent number of pheasants that season and when it was over I once again sold him on. At this stage there was another great debate going on, between Catch and myself, regarding the best way to find a "good Dog". Catch had always been of the opinion that money solves all problems and his answer has always been to pay a decent price for a mature working dog, where performance can be ascertained before you part with any cash.

My problem with this is, that you then end up with a dog that is capable of working by himself but not really in tune with his master. The problem with buying a pup, on the other hand, is that at least two seasons are lost before you know one way or the other.

During the seasons of 1995 and 1996 we debated this thorny issue at every opportunity, without ever really resolving it. Life had changed somewhat for me and I was now quite reluctant to start with a pup. The commitment of time is two-fold. Firstly there is all the training which I find very time-consuming nowadays and also, after the loss of my long term shooting partner, there is the real difficulty about committing to another ten years or more of the sport.

As the 1997 season approached, I was in a somewhat happier position, in that I had teamed up with a new partner, Willie Hibbits. We had shot together many times over the years, although we had each had our own partners, and now he had a dog and no partner, so for a time I thought that all my problems were solved. However, the first of the season was yet again a bit of a disappointment. Willie had to work on the day, so Catch and myself got together and used his dog. The old problem of not knowing the dog, coupled with the fact that the dog was mediocre meant that by the end of the day we had shot two cocks, but we both knew that it was more through luck than good shooting. Or rather, good dog-work. As dusk fell that evening, we were in the car driving along the lane that led from our old friend Sean Quinn's farm. We were both heavy of heart as well as tired and, when Catch spoke there was a finality about his voice.

In essence what he said was, that the sport of shooting had been good to us for close on forty years and that what we were doing now was little more than a mockery. "Either we get decent dogs before next year or we give it up altogether". At that, we shook hands and I wondered seriously was this for the last time in a shooting context. I decided there and then that, if I was ever to write this book, that the time was now. The following day, I purchased a hard-backed note book, a ruler and two pens. That night, I set about putting a lifetime of memories down in some kind of order. By a strange coincidence, Catch phoned me that same night to say that he had been given an option on a pointer pup. He was excited and full of talk about the possibilities that this new canine might offer. I pointed out, however, that all this was still two years down the line. A week later, he phoned again to say that he had bought a four-and-a-half-year-old pointer, a working dog and he wanted me to come at once to Limerick to see him in action.

I did, and fell in love with him from the start. The fact that Catch already had a pup meant that he would sell the older dog at the end of the season and so, it came to pass that on the first Sunday in February I again went to Limerick to take possession of my new dog, " Bonzo". All in all, a strange state of affairs. Catch training a pup, me buying a mature dog and writing a book at the same time. Wonders will never cease. Now, as I write these final chapters, it is December 2000. In the meantime, we have enjoyed two more great seasons and, this one is shaping up well, despite the weather. The fields are muddy and wet beyond belief, the drains are full to overflowing, the pheasants are as wild and scarce as ever at Christmas and I'm loving every minute of it.

Back cover. The poacher's view.

EPILOGUE

The writing of this book has truly been a labour of love. The word labour coming, not only from the long hours spent at the word processor while the rest of the world carried on gaily without me. But also from the fact that, as a child of the fifties and sixties, I had to embrace this new technology. I had to learn to type, edit text, format it, use "cut and paste" and click on all sorts of icons. In short, I had to master the computer. I feel pleased with the results from that perspective.

The part which I loved was, having to recall the fun and good-times of a lifetime. Memories which still warm the cockles of my heart, but also sadly, leave me and other field-sports enthusiasts at odds with those who seek a more "politically correct" society.

Many people recoil in horror at the thought of somebody taking pleasure in hunting. They say that we no longer need to hunt for food and that therefore the practice should be consigned to the history books. By that logic should sex also be discarded, given that we can now procreate artificially?.

Food is the only commodity which Mankind must partake of. Every day we eat meat, which has been farmed specifically for the table, some in very natural conditions. More of it, and I am thinking of pigs and poultry in particular are reared in deplorable conditions. People eat fish fingers, without ever seeming to realise that fish do not have fingers at all, but rather heads and tails. Tons of sea-fish are trawled from the seas and left to suffocate, without any thought for the cruelty involved. Many of them are gutted while still alive.

The game, which I hunt, invariably ends up being

greatly revered at the table. Either by myself, or having been given as a treasured gift to appreciative friends. That same game may have had a short life. But it will have been happy, in its own natural environment, well fed and cared for and given relative protection from predators. It saddens me greatly to think that the world, in which I grew up, is probably gone forever.

Lest anyone think that I am trying to turn the world into a race of vegetarians, just imagine what would happen if we did. The land would be tilled and used to grow all the grain and vegetables required, to feed our ever burgeoning millions. What would become of all the cattle, pigs, sheep and hens? The vegetarians' answer must surely be to eradicate them, given that we would no longer have any need, or room, for them.

Ireland has become a more urban environment and very few children have the same ready access to the wide, open countryside. But, even those who do are all too often caught up in the instant gratification that goes with the electronic age. Videos and computer games are more appealing to the new generation. Only recently, we had "Jackie and Daw" on the internet. Educational it may have been, but how sad to think that so few children feel the need to find birds' nests for themselves anymore.

My abiding love of nature was fashioned and forged during my formative years. Those childhood memories can still enrich and enhance my daily life some forty years later. The intervening years have been but a river of complementary experiences.

Whenever I reminisce, I only occasionally remember wonderful shooting days, when many birds were shot, or even the well taken and therefore more pleasing shots. I prefer to think of the partners with whom I shared the pleasure. Also, I remember the countless hours spent alone and at peace with nature. I remember the various dogs, which it has been my great pleasure and privilege to own and work with. I frequently recall the September days when I encountered clutches of young pheasants and saw them erupt like fireworks from under the nose of a young and very excited pup. I recall those same young dogs maturing and learning their craft to perfection. The sight of a dog doing his job is as pleasing to watch, as any master craftsman at work. That unique sense of teamwork, when man and animal combine to produce the game.

I remember also the hollow mocking sound of heavy wing-beats echoing through a frozen wood, as a cute old cock evaded capture, and wondering if I will get another chance before the season ends. Or the proud crow of a cock in early summer, telling me that all is well with the world and that his mate is happily brooding away, preparing the new harvest. Above all, I think about some of the characters which this great sport has given me the pleasure of knowing. Simple country folk, many of whom live alone, and who actively look forward to contact with shooting men. Their lives, in many cases, seemingly untouched by modernisation. People who were happy the way they were and who want to make time stand still forever. I love them.